TWILIGHT OF THE SOCIAL

Copyright © 2012 Paradigm Publishers

Published in the United States by Paradigm Publishers, 2845 Wilderness Place, Boulder, CO 80301 USA.

Paradigm Publishers is the trade name of Birkenkamp & Company, LLC, Dean Birkenkamp, President and Publisher.

Library of Congress Cataloging-in-Publication data
Giroux, Henry A.
   Twilight of the social : resurgent publics in the age of disposability / Henry A. Giroux.
      p. cm.
   Includes bibliographical references and index.
   ISBN 978-1-61205-055-3 (hbk. : alk. paper) —
ISBN 978-1-61205-056-0 (pbk. : alk. paper)
   1. United States—Social conditions—1980- 2. United States—Social policy—1993- 3. United States—Politics and government—2009- I. Title.
   HN59.2.G556 2012
   303.450973'09051—dc23
                                                     2011031841

Printed and bound in the United States of America on acid-free paper that meets the standards of the American National Standard for Permanence of Paper for Printed Library Materials.

Designed and Typeset by Straight Creek Bookmakers.

16 15 14 13 12   1 2 3 4 5

TWILIGHT OF THE SOCIAL
RESURGENT PUBLICS
IN THE AGE OF DISPOSABILITY

HENRY A. GIROUX

Paradigm Publishers
Boulder • London

For Susan
For Subhash Dighe

◇

Contents

◇

Acknowledgments

This book would not have been completed on time without the help of many friends who offered invaluable criticisms and support. I would like to especially thank Roger Simon, Donaldo Macedo, and David Theo Goldberg. I am deeply indebted to Grace Pollock, my research assistant, who once again provided detailed editorial suggestions on the entire manuscript, while greatly improving the quality of the overall project. I also want to think Maya Sabados whose skills and help went far beyond any standard measure of excellence. She read each chapter, helped enormously in organizing research notes, and provided much needed support. Susan Searls Giroux took time out of her own busy schedule to read the manuscript, offer a number of important insights, and perform her usual editorial magic. I also want to thank Victoria Harper, my editor at *Truthout*, for giving me the opportunity to publish some of these pieces. I also want to thank Michael Peters for reprinting a few of these essays in *Policy Futures in Education*. I also want to extend my deepest appreciation to Dean Birkenkamp, my friend and editor at Paradigm Publishers, for encouraging me to produce this book.

An earlier version of Chapter One was published as "Neoliberalism and the Death of the Social State: Remembering Walter Benjamin's Angel of History," *Social Identities* 17:4 (July 2011), pp. 587–601. A version of Chapter Two, "The Crisis of Public Values in the Age of the New Media," was published in *Critical Studies in Media Communication*, 28:1 (2011), pp. 8–29.

◇

INTRODUCTION

Left Behind?

American Youth and the Global Fight for Democracy

[O]ne has no choice but to do all in one's power to change that fate [of class and racial oppression], and at no matter what risk—eviction, imprisonment, torture, death. For the sake of one's children, in order to minimize the bill that they must pay, one must be careful not to take refuge in any delusion.

—*James Baldwin*[1]

The people have awakened. If change had happened through elites, there wouldn't have been real change. Now people understand their rights and know how to demand them. They realized their own power.

—*Ahmed Mahir, leader of the Egyptian Youth April 6th Movement*

Within the last year, we have seen an outpouring of student protests from all over the globe. Fifty thousand students took to the streets in London to protest tuition hikes, and "thousands of young people in Puerto Rico and Ireland are marching against cuts to student funding and fee increases."[2] Students in France and Greece are demonstrating with their bodies, confronting the police, and registering their outrage over the imposition of severe austerity measures. In Spain and Italy, youth are challenging unemployment rates that

1

have soared to 40 and 30 percent, respectively. In Tunisia and Egypt, students have been at the forefront of uprisings that eventually led to the overthrow of authoritarian societies, which for too long forced young people to linger in a liminal space in which there were no jobs, no hope for the future, and far too few freedoms. In Syria and Libya, young people are literally dying because of their brave efforts to reform deeply authoritarian societies. This general sense of frustration among young people is widespread in Europe and the Middle East. For instance, students marching in Rome "shouted, 'We don't want to pay for the crisis,' referring to the financial crisis that has turned ... labor market[s] from bad to worse. 'Where do I see my future? Certainly not in this country,' said protester, Morgana Proietti, expressing a common sentiment."[3]

Counter-public spheres and modes of resistance that we once did not think young people could mount have erupted in a rush of emotional and political expressions and scattered demonstrations. Mass demonstrations have been organized through the emergent screen cultures of a generation well versed in new technologically assisted forms of social networking and political exchange. Governments complicit with a lethal combination of massive inequality, joblessness, and ongoing cutbacks in social services are now the object of righteous youthful aggression in which buildings are occupied, pitched battles are waged in the streets, banners are dropped from national symbols like the Leaning Tower of Pisa, and once impregnable governmental institutions are subject to intense criticism. Shared sufferings, pent up repressions, ideological longings, and emotional attachments have flared up in a massive collective demand by young people to be part of a future in which justice, democratic values, and politics once again matter. Forging collective spaces of resistance, young people are expressing their long-simmering anger and indignation against harsh injustices, growing inequalities, and insufferable injuries in both totalitarian and allegedly democratic countries. The fear of political transgression and the ensuing repression that kept individual actors in check has given way to a politics in which dissent is amplified, multiplied, and seized upon with a vigor and moral courage that has seldom found such thunderous expression among young people since the late 1970s. Democracy is no longer being defended. It is being reinvented as a kind of shared existence that makes the political possible.[4]

Moral outrage infused by a complex of affective connections, social despair, and a deeply held sense of shared possibilities has created a spontaneous tsunami of collective protests, strikes, rallies, and demonstrations that have toppled governments, prompted shameless retaliatory outbursts of state terrorism, and further fueled the possibilities for a global sense of resistance among repressed youth everywhere. Young people have used the new media to mobilize mass demonstrations, pitting their bodies against the police, army, and other repressive forces. But they have also used the Internet and various social networks such as Twitter and Facebook to reach across national boundaries. In doing so, they have shared experiences, gathered information, circulated strategies for dealing with the police, and developed nonviolent modes of protest.[5] For example, young leaders in Egypt exchanged information "with similar youth movements in Libya, Algeria, and Morocco and Iran."[6]

Signaling a generational crisis that is global in scope, young people have sent a message to the world that they refuse to live any longer under repressive political regimes sustained by a morally bankrupt neoliberal world. Throughout Europe, youth exercised their sense of collective agency by calling for a revision of how democracy both listens to and treats them. In doing so, they disrupted the neoliberal inclination to take flight from social and moral responsibility. They defied a social order in which they could not find employment, have access to a quality education, or support a family, a social order that offered them only a life stripped of self-determination and dignity. A generation that was viewed as no longer having or caring about the future decided to abandon whatever residual faith they might have had in official politics. And for those who had no faith in the first place, their lot was a depoliticizing cynicism that often accompanies a loss of hope in the future. In an outburst that indicted the lack of vision, courage, and responsibility on the part of their elders, young people in Egypt, Libya, Tunisia, France, Puerto Rico, and Greece took history into their own hands. They were fighting not merely for a space to survive, but for a society in which matters of justice, dignity, and freedom are objects of collective struggle. These uprisings signal a new stage in which young people are once again defining what John Pilger calls the "theater of the possible."[7] The shimmering fantasy, if not illusion and banalization, of hope gave way to a politics of collective action and massive resistance. From Tunis to Paris, a politics emerged that revealed a longing for the not-yet-and-still-possible. Although marked by different historical contexts and diverse problems, this is a new kind of global politics in which the promise of democracy is reclaimed as a site of resistance, rather than being used as either a hypocritical slogan for defending a repressive status quo or an empty appeasement promoting endless deferral of the promise of a better life. Students in western Europe, in particular, are doing more than protesting cuts in educational funding and higher tuition rates; they are also loudly rejecting the market-driven insistence that education neither qualifies as a public good nor should it be valued as a democratic public sphere. Nina Power, one of the student protestors in London, makes this clear in a comment reported in *The Guardian*. She insisted that, "It was a protest against the narrowing of horizons; a protest against Lib Dem hypocrisy; a protest against the increasingly utilitarian approach to human life that sees degrees as nothing but 'investments' by individuals, and denies any link between education and the broader social good."[8] Giuliano Amato, a former Italian prime minister, in an interview with the country's largest newspaper, *Corriere della Sera*, makes clear that what students are protesting against involves more than economic issues. As he puts it, "they are also against a general situation in which the older generations have eaten the future of the younger ones."[9]

As I write this, massive looting and acts of violence are taking place in London. While it is easy to dismiss these expressions of violence and law-breaking as criminal acts, the conditions that fuel them are deeply political and economic and speak to how youth have been abandoned under neoliberal regimes.

Underlying these youth protests in various countries is a set of conditions that reflects differing economic and political contexts. Yet, at the same time, many of these nations share a disdain for young people and a not-too-hidden willingness to take advantage of any youth who are deemed valuable, leaving the rest to be increasingly viewed as troublemakers and subject to a growing apparatus of discipline and control.

Under the global regime of a harsh, endlessly commodifying market-driven society that nonetheless parades under the banner of global democratization, many youth are confined to what anthropologist Joao Biehl provocatively calls "zones of social abandonment."[10] These expanding groups of young people, especially those marginalized by class, race, and immigrant status, are defined as a liability, no longer worthy of either social investment or the promise of a decent future. They are deprived of those autonomous social spaces in which the conditions exist for them to narrate themselves as individual and social agents. Meanwhile, politics under neoliberalism has been redefined through the double registers of corruption and punishment—not behind people's backs, as Marx once supposed it, but in full spectacular view of the world.

Out of place and subject to a grating diversity of realities that reveal massive unemployment, underpaid temporary work, skyrocketing tuition, escalating rent, rising food costs, deepening poverty, and the indignity of having to live with their parents indefinitely, youth no longer symbolize one of the most crucial investments enabling a society to build on its dreams. On the contrary, placed at the limits of the social, youth have become as Jean and John Comaroff point out "the creatures of our nightmares, of our social impossibilities and our existential angst."[11] Moreover, any expression of dissent invites state sanctioned rage, violence, torture, and imprisonment. Both banned and abandoned by society, too many young people around the globe now live in what Zygmunt Bauman calls "a state of perpetual emergency."[12]

Every generation for the last thirty years has endorsed neoliberal policies, leaving today's young people not only without a voice, but also saddled with a set of economic, political, and social conditions that have rendered them devalued, marginalized, and ultimately disposable. Evidence of the ongoing disinvestment in youth across the globe is all too visible and has come to the forefront of student protests in a number of countries. For example, as the social value placed on higher education as a public good declines, students are increasingly valued, when valued at all, as wage earners. This is rather ironic, because there are few jobs for them to choose from once they graduate. That the forces at work in capitalist countries—whether putatively democratic or overtly authoritarian—deny young people a future can be seen in a litany of disheartening figures. Elias Holtz sums it up well:

> In capitalist countries worldwide, young people are sand-wiched between the increasingly impossible expense of schooling and the dried-up job market. Youth unemployment rates are staggering. They are above 40 percent in Spain, 30 percent in Italy and an average of 20 percent for the European Union overall. In North Africa, unemployment of recent university graduates is almost 27 percent in Morocco and over 19 percent in Algeria. A third of all Arab youth are un-employed.... Corporations and employers have also moved to a more exploitative model of temporary work contracts, unpaid internships, and part-time employment. This liquid-izes the young labor force, allowing companies to hire and fire at will, without the responsibility of providing job security or benefits. Many young people are forced to live at home in rich countries—unable to afford to live independently. In poorer states, they peddle goods on the street to survive.[13]

In countries like the United States, driven largely by financial speculation, market values, and the lure of short-term profits, young people are relegated to the status of commodities, a source of cheap labor, or simply human waste. How else to explain right-wing politicians in the United States arguing for legislation that would repeal child labor laws,[14] reduce food stamps, cut medical assistance, and limit educational opportunities "available to poor children"?[15] It gets worse. As Abby Zimet points out: "Michigan's GOP lawmakers want to close a $1.4 billion deficit and fund $1.8 billion in business tax cuts. They propose to do this by cutting disability assistance, early childhood funding, and indigent burial expenses and requiring foster children to spend their $79 clothing allowance only at second-hand stores. This might save as much as $200,000, and thus our national economy and the world as we know it."[16] According to the logic of neoliberalism and what can only be described as its perversion of the social, youth as a long-term social investment fails to register politically or ethically. Instead, young people exist—if it can be called an existence—merely as consumers, clients, or fodder for the military and prison-industrial complex. Or, as in the previous example of economically underprivileged foster children, young people when weighed against the interests of the rich and powerful are viewed as merely disposable.

As more and more young people are subject to the dictates of the punishing state, they are positioned within a culture of surveillance and cruelty marked by dead time. Futureless, they have been stuck in holding patterns that make it clear that the United States's market-driven economy is deeply disconnected from humanity's collective relationship and responsibility to youth and the future.[17] Young people for the last three decades in a variety of Western societies have been led to believe that their choices no longer carry any serious consequences and that a better future is no longer open to them. As Lawrence Grossberg argues, youth have been condemned to "a new modernity in which there can be only one kind of value, market value; one kind of success, profit; one kind of existence, commodities; and one kind of social relationship, markets."[18]

The global recession has intensified the war on youth, as professionals and politicians who make up a global business class now displace democracy with the call for austerity and, in doing so, produce a hidden order of politics in which the "demand for the people's austerity hides processes of the uneven distribution of risk and vulnerability."[19] Under the guise of austerity, politically motivated attacks are now being waged on a generation of young people, African Americans, unions, workers, and the elderly. On the other hand, austerity measures against the rich are almost nonexistent. Richard D. Wolff provides the details in looking at what he calls "some alternative 'reasonable' kinds of austerity." He writes:

> Serious efforts to collect income taxes from U.S.-based multinational corporations, especially those who use internal pricing mechanisms to escape U.S. taxation, would generate vast new federal revenues. The same applies to wealthy individuals. The U.S. has no federal property tax on holdings of stocks, bonds, and cash accounts (states and localities levy no such property taxes either). If the federal government levied a 1 per cent tax on assets between $100,000 to 499,000, and 1.5 per cent on assets above $500,000, that would raise much new federal revenue (everyone's first $100,000 could be exempted just as the existing U.S. income tax exempts the first few thousands of dollars of individual incomes). Exiting

the Iraq and Afghanistan disasters would do likewise. Ending tax exemptions for super-rich private educational institutions (Harvard, Yale, etc.) and for religious institutions (church-goers would then need to pay the costs of their churches) would be among the many other such alternative "reasonable" austerity measures. Comparable alternatives apply—and are being struggled over—in other countries.[20]

Instead, the mode of austerity boldly enacted in the United States entails what I call the politics of trickle-down cruelty. This is evident in policies in which austerity-based cuts are used to reward corporations and billionaires with tax breaks while simultaneously exploiting the budget crisis in order to eliminate protections provided by the welfare state. The resulting reductions in state spending have drastically cut many basic social services so as to endanger the lives of many young people and others at the margins of a society structured by massive financial inequality. For example, in Philadelphia, "fire departments have been closed on a daily rotating basis" delaying response time. One unfortunate and possibly preventable consequence occurred "when two children were pulled from a burning row home too little too late.... Mike Kane of the Philadelphia Firefighters Union Local 22 said there was no way to tell whether the children would have lived had the fire station been open, but if not for the brownouts, 'maybe them kids would have had a shot.'"[21] In Arizona, Governor Jan Brewer signed a bill that effec-tively denied health care to more than 47,000 low-income children.[22] Austerity in this instance is designed to reward the fabulously wealthy while imposing in some cases pov-erty, suffering, and severe hardship on those marginalized by race, disability, and class. For many young people, these examples suggest that the writing is on the wall regarding their future and the message is dark indeed. Both neoliberal-driven governments and authoritarian societies share one important factor: They care more about consolidating power in the hands of a political, corporate, and financial elite than they do about investing in the future of young people. And it is precisely a struggle over the future that is at the center of a new global youth movement.

What is new in these youth revolts that are rewriting the politics of the Middle East and western Europe is a refusal on the part of young people to be written out of the future. The violence of the neoliberal state and its antidemocratic and authoritarian articulations reveals a politics in which young people are labeled as an apathetic generation, comfortable with living in a "state of stupor, in a moral coma," in order to justify denying their basic needs and forcing them to bear the brunt of the dynamics of ruthless economic institutions working along with a growing culture of cruelty.[23] The culture of opportunity and ideals of social justice endemic to a democratic society have been transformed into the mechanizations of a foreclosure and punishing society. Under these circumstances, there has been a concerted effort on the part of authoritarian and corporate states to destroy all those democratic public spheres that enable new models of association. Such models of association are considered dangerous because they offer the promise of educating people about how the capitalist system works while at the same time injecting back into the public imagination a notion of social change that allows for structural transformation. If young people are granted the time, resources, and support to reclaim a future that does not imitate the present, these models will have a better chance at creating the conditions for a future that makes good on the ideals and promises of democratization. What is remarkable about the mass revolts in Europe and the Middle East today is that young people have taken the lead in rejecting a future, which, for the last thirty years or more, has been shamelessly mortgaged by both Western countries, embracing a form of zombie politics and economic Darwinism, and authoritarian Middle Eastern societies that exhibit a deep hatred for democracy.

After living through years of a debilitating and humiliating disinvestment in the future, young people have hit the streets to reject the dismantling of services provided by the social state, the selling off of public goods, the politics of unchecked individualism, the rise of the punishing state, the collapse of long-term planning for the social good, and the all-encompassing and iniquitous power of corporate and authoritarian modes of sovereignty. At the heart of the emergent struggles we are witnessing all over the globe are youth movements that refuse to be silent and are more than willing to shatter, as Jacques Rancière puts it, the "coordinates of the sensible [and] bonds that enclose spectacles ... within the machine that makes the 'state of things' unquestionable."[24] Students and young people are now fighting back, affirming new modes of solidarity, forming alliances with workers and labor organizations, and embracing a vision of democracy committed to economic and political equality. Most remarkably, this new generation of young people is able not only to think in terms that relate isolated problems to larger public considerations, but also to recognize the importance of a civic society that provides the formative culture necessary for self-governing democratic societies. Hence, the emphasis on the new media, social networks, and the Internet is not merely about dodging the repression of dissent. It is more importantly about creating alternative public spheres where the values, ideas, dialogue, knowledge, and social relations necessary for a democracy can take root, if not flourish.[25] It is about creating counter-public spheres that "assert the public character of spaces, relations, and institutions regarded as private" or currently limited to members of the ruling classes and authoritarian elites.[26] This is a generation that is fighting back and, in doing so, inventing new pedagogical tools to expose the official scripts of power while at the same time constructing new modes of association and struggle based on democratic ideals and values. One fifteen-year-old student speaking at a London youth conference captures the spirit of what it means for his generation to challenge contemporary injustices and inequality:

> We were meant to be the first post-ideological generation, right? ... That never thought of anything bigger than our Facebook profiles and TV screens.... I think now that claim is quite ridiculous, now we've shown that solidarity and comradeship and all those things that used to be associated with students are as relevant now as they've ever been. We are now the generation at the heart of the fight-back.[27]

What is promising about these student protests is that, although they might have begun in relation to specific issues, such as rising tuition costs or mass unemployment, they have gained momentum and successfully mobilized other constituencies, such as labor, by connecting single issues to a wider set of economic, social, and political conditions. In doing so, these new social movements have called the larger neoliberal Zeitgeist into question. Specific issues have given rise to broader considerations. As a result, the totality of neoliberal and totalitarian societies has begun to fragment and weaken, offering a space for a broad alliance of individuals and groups who are seeking not only political reform but also meaningful and pervasive ideological and structural changes. Increasingly, in the West, especially in Greece, France, and other countries on the verge of financial default, students, workers, and intellectuals are not only questioning the market-driven policies of neoliberalism but raising important questions about the possible alternatives to capitalism itself.

In the face of the mass uprisings in western Europe and the Middle East, many commentators have raised questions about why comparable forms of widespread resistance are not taking place among U.S. youth. Everyone from left critics to mainstream radio commentators voice surprise and disappointment that U.S. youth appear unengaged by the collective action their counterparts in other countries are participating in and promoting. Courtney Martin, a senior correspondent for *The American Prospect,* suggests that U.S. students are often privileged and view politics as something that happens elsewhere, far removed from local activism.[28] She writes:

> Those who are politically active tend to set their sights on distant horizons—the poor in India, say, or the oppressed in Afghanistan.... Many of us from middle- and upper-income backgrounds have been socialized to believe that it is our duty to make a difference, but undertake such efforts abroad—where the "real" poor people are. We found nonprofits aimed at schooling children all over the globe while rarely acknowledging that our friend from the high school football team can't afford the same kind of opportunities we can. Or we create Third World bicycle programs while ignoring that our lab partner has to travel two hours by bus, as he is unable to get a driver's license as an undocumented immigrant. We were born lucky, so we head to the bars—oblivious to the rising tuition prices and crushing bureaucracy inside the financial aid office.[29]

The other side of the overprivileged youth argument is suggested by longtime activist Tom Hayden, who argues that many students are so saddled with financial debt and focused on what it takes to get a job that they have little time for political activism.[30] Either way, student activism in the United States, especially since the 1980s, has been narrowly issues-based, ranging from a focus on student unionization, gender equity, environmental issues, and greater minority enrollment to "the establishment of ethnic studies programs in universities or health-care benefits for graduate students," thus circumscribing in advance youth participation in larger political spheres.[31] Simon Talley, a writer for *Campus Progress,* might be closer to the truth in claiming that students in the United States have less of an investment in higher education than European students because for the last thirty years they have been told that higher education neither serves a public good nor is an invaluable democratic public sphere.[32]

These commentators, along with many others, all underestimate the historical and current impacts of the conservative political climate on U.S. campuses on the culture of youth protest. This conservatism took firm hold with the election of Ronald Reagan and the emergence of both neoconservative and neoliberal disciplinary apparatuses since the 1970s.[33] Youth have in fact been very active in the last few decades, but in many instances for deeply conservative ends. As Susan Searls Giroux has effectively argued, a series of well-funded, right-wing campus organizations have made much use of old and new media to produce best-selling screeds as well as interactive websites for students to report injustices in the interests of protesting the alleged left-totalitarianism of the academy:

> Conservative think tanks provide $20 million annually to the campus Right, according to the People for the American Way, to fund campus organizations such as Students for Academic Freedom, whose credo is "You can't get a good education if they're only telling you half the story" and boasts over 150 campus chapters. Providing an online complaint form for disgruntled students to fill out, the organization's website monitors insults, slurs and claims of more serious infractions that students claim to have suffered. Similarly, the Intercollegiate Studies Institute, founded by William F. Buckley, funds

over 80 right-wing student publications through its Collegiate Network, which has produced such media darlings as Dinesh D'Souza and Ann Coulter. There is also the Leadership Institute, which trains, supports and does public relations for 213 conservative student groups who are provided with suggestions for inviting conservative speakers to campus, help starting conservative newspapers, or training to win campus elections. Then there is the Young Americans for Freedom, which sponsors various campus activities such as "affirmative action bake sales" where students are charged variously according to their race or ethnicity, or announcements of "whites only" scholarships.[34]

Liberal students, for their part, have engaged in forms of activism that also mimic neoliberal rationalities. The increasing emphasis on consumerism, instant gratification, and the narcissistic ethic of privatization took its toll in a range of student protests developed over issues such as the right to party and "a defense of the right to consume alcohol." As Mark Edelman Boren points out in his informative book on student resistance, alcohol-related issues caused student uprisings on a number of U.S. campuses. In one telling example, he writes, "At Ohio University, several thousand students rioted in April 1998 for a second annual violent protest over the loss of an hour of drinking when clocks were officially set back at the beginning of daylight savings time; forced out of area bars, upset students hurled rocks and bottles at police, who knew to show up in full riot gear after the previous year's riot. The troops finally resorted to shooting wooden 'knee-knocker' bullets at the rioters to suppress them."[35]

All of these explanations have some merit in accounting for the lack of student resistance among U.S. students, but I'd like to shift the focus of this conversation. Student resistance in the United States must be viewed within a broader political landscape that, with few exceptions, remains unexamined. In the first instance, students in western Europe, in particular, are faced with a series of crises that are more immediate, bold, and radical in their assault on young people and the institutions that bear down heavily on their lives. In the face of the economic recession, educational budgets are being cut in take-no-prisoners extreme fashion, the social state is being radically dismantled, tuition costs have spiked exponentially, and unemployment rates for young people are far higher than in the United States (with the exception of youth in poor minority communities). European students have experienced a massive and bold assault on their lives, educational opportunities, and their future. Moreover, European students live in societies where it becomes more difficult to collapse public life into largely private considerations. Students in these countries have access to a wider range of critical public spheres; politics in many of these countries has not collapsed entirely into the spectacle of celebrity/commodity culture; left-oriented political parties still exist; and labor unions have more political and ideological clout than they do in the United States. Alternative newspapers, progressive media, and a profound sense of the political constitute elements of a vibrant, critical, formative culture and range of public spheres that have not erased the possibility to think critically, engage in political dissent, organize collectively, and inhabit public spaces in which alternative and critical theories can be developed.

Because of the diverse nature of how higher education is financed and governed in the United States, the assault on colleges and universities has been less uniform and differentially spread out among community colleges, public universities, and elite colleges, thus lacking a unified and highly oppressive narrative against which to position resistance. Moreover, the campus "culture wars" narrative has served to galvanize many youth around a reactionary cultural project, while distancing them from the very nature of the economic and political assault on their future. All this suggests that another set of questions has to be raised. The more important questions, ones that do not reproduce the all-too-commonplace demonization of young people as apathetic, are twofold. First, the issue should not be why there have been no student protests, but why have the protests that have happened not been more widespread, linked, sustained? The student protest against the draconian right-wing policies attempting to destroy the union rights and collective bargaining power of teachers supported by Republican Governor Scott Walker in Wisconsin is one example indicating that students are engaged and concerned. There are also smaller student protests taking place at various colleges, including

Berkeley, the City University of New York, and other campuses throughout the United States. But student activists appear to constitute a minority of students, with very few enrolled in professional programs. Most student activists are coming from the arts, social sciences, and humanities (the conscience of the college). Second, there is the crucial issue of what sort of conditions young people have inherited in U.S. society that have undermined their ability to be critical agents capable of waging a massive protest movement against the growing injustices they face on a daily basis. After all, the assault on higher education in the United States, although not as severe as those in Europe, still suggests ample reason for students to be in the streets protesting such policies. Close to forty-three states have pledged major cuts to higher education in order to compensate for insufficient state funding. This means an unprecedented hike in tuition rates is being implemented; enrollments are being slashed; salaries are being reduced; and need-based scholarships in some states are being eliminated. Pell Grants, which allow poor students to attend college, are being cut. Robert Reich has chronicled some of the impacts on university budgets, which include: Georgia cutting "state funding for higher education by $151 million," Michigan reducing "student financial aid by $135 million,"[36] Florida raising tuition in its eleven public universities by 15 percent, and the University of California increasing tuition by 40 percent in two years.[37] As striking as these increases are, tuition has steadily risen over the past several decades, becoming a disturbingly normative feature of postsecondary education.

One reason students are not protesting these cuts in larger numbers might be that by the time the average U.S. student graduates, he or she has not only a degree but also an average debt of about $23,000.[38] The vast majority must balance jobs with academics, leaving no opportunity to protest, however motivated a student might be. This debt amounts to a growing form of indentured servitude for many students that undercuts any viable notion of social activism and is exacerbated by the fact that "unemployment for recent college graduates jumped from 5.8 percent to 8.7 percent in 2009."[39] Crippling debt plus few job opportunities in a society in which individuals are relentlessly held as solely responsible for the problems they experience leaves little room for rethinking the importance of larger social issues and the necessity for organized collective action against systemic injustices. In addition, as higher education becomes one of the most fundamental requirements for employment, many universities have reconfigured their mission exclusively in corporate terms, replacing education with training and defining students as consumers, faculty as a cheap form of subaltern labor, and entire academic departments as "cost centers and revenue production units."[40] No longer seen as a social or public good, higher education is increasingly viewed less as a site of struggle than as a credential mill for success in the global economy.

Meanwhile, not only have academic jobs been disappearing, but, given the shift to an instrumentalist education that is technicist in nature, students have been confronted for quite some time with a vanishing culture for sustained critical thinking. As universities and colleges emphasize market-based skills, students are learning neither how to think critically nor how to connect private troubles with larger public issues. The humanities continue to be downsized, eliminating one source of learning that encourages students to develop a commitment to public values, social responsibilities, and the broader demands of critical citizenship. Moreover, critical thinking has been devalued as a result of the growing corporatization of higher education. Under the influence of corporate values, thought, in its most operative sense, loses its modus operandi as a critical mediation on "civilization, existence, and forms of evaluation."[41] Increasingly, it has become more difficult for students to recognize how their education in the broadest sense has been systematically devalued, and how this not only undercuts their ability to be engaged critics but contributes further to making U.S. democracy dysfunctional. How else to explain the reticence of students toward protesting in large numbers against tuition hikes? The forms of instrumental training they receive undermine any critical capacity to connect the fees they pay to the fact that the United States puts more money into the funding of war, armed forces, and military weaponry than the next twenty-five countries combined— money that could otherwise fund higher education.[42] In a society where knowledge is instrumentalized, commodified, fragmented, and privatized, it becomes difficult for everyone, not just students, to connect private troubles to public problems. For instance, the U.S. government has no qualms "in spending $20.2 billion a year for air-conditioning the troops in Iraq and Afghanistan."[43] Yet, warmongering politicians are indifferent to the fact that the same amount of money could be used to fill the $20 billion shortfall in the Pell Grant Program mentioned previously. Such figures point to the need to connect the call for educational and social reform to sharp reductions in the military budget and to negotiate an end to the permanent warfare state.

The inability to be critical of such injustices and to relate them to a broader understanding of politics suggests a failure to think outside of the normative sensibilities of a neoliberal ideology that instrumentalizes knowledge and normalizes its own power relations. In fact, one recent study found that "45 percent of students show no significant improvement in the key measures of critical thinking, complex reasoning and writing by the end of their sophomore years."[44] The corporatization of schooling over the last few decades has done more than make universities into adjuncts of corporate power. It has also produced a culture of illiteracy and undermined the conditions necessary to enable students to be engaged and critical agents. The value of knowledge is now linked to a crude instrumentalism, and the only mode of education that seems to matter is one that enthusiastically endorses learning marketable skills, embracing a survival-of-the-fittest ethic, and defining the good life solely through accumulation and disposing of the latest consumer goods. Academic knowledge has been stripped of its value as a social good; to be relevant and therefore funded, knowledge has to justify itself in market terms, or simply perish.

Enforced privatization, the closing down of critical public spheres, and the endless commodification of all aspects of social life have created a generation of students who are increasingly being reared in a society in which politics is viewed as irrelevant, just as the struggle for democracy is erased from social memory. This is not to suggest that Americans have abandoned the notion that ideas have power or that ideologies and visions can move people. Unfortunately, the institutions and cultural apparatuses that generate such ideas seem to be primarily controlled by the corporate media, right-wing think tanks, and other conservative groups.

Public pedagogy is dominated by the right, whose activities proceed more often than not unchallenged from a left that has never taken public pedagogy seriously as part of its political strategy. The rise of the Tea Party movement seems to have no counterpart among progressives, especially young people, although this might change, given the arrogant and right-wing attack being waged on unions, public sector workers, and public school educators in Wisconsin, Florida, Georgia, Ohio, New Jersey, and other states where putative Tea Party candidates have come to power.[45]

In a social order dominated by the relentless privatizing and commodification of everyday life and the elimination of critical public spheres, young people find themselves in a society in which the formative cultures necessary for a democracy to exist have been more or less eliminated, reduced to spectacles of consumerism, made palatable through a daily diet of game shows, reality TV, and celebrity culture. What is particularly troubling in U.S. society is the absence of vital formative cultures necessary to construct questioning agents who are capable of seeing through the consumer come-ons, who can dissent and act collectively in an increasingly imperiled democracy. As young people are reared in a society in which hope is privatized and the ethical imagination tranquilized, it becomes difficult to assume responsibility for the other or to imagine politics as a site to sustain a sense of justice and collective responsibility for the common good.

As education is reduced to the instrumental dictates of a business culture and other critical public spheres are commercialized, it has become more and more difficult for young people to inhabit those public spaces that enable them to think critically, make informed judgments, and distinguish cogent arguments from mere opinions. Moreover, as the new media and screen culture become the quintessential space of representation and entertainment in late capitalism, there is not only an overflow of information but the emergence of new forms of illiteracy in which many young people cannot focus very long on specific tasks or connect discrete pieces of information to larger narratives and increasingly view information as a commodity limited to privatizing pursuits. The delete button has replaced the critical knowledge and the modes of education needed for intimacy, long-term commitments, and the search for the good society. Attachments are short-lived, and the pleasure of instant gratification cancels out the coupling of freedom, reason, and responsibility. As a long-term social investment, young people are now viewed as a liability, if not a pathology. No longer a symbol of hope and the future, they are viewed as a drain on the economy, and if they do not assume the role of functioning consumers or potential recruits for the war machine, they are considered disposable.

Within the last thirty years, the United States, under the reign of market fundamentalism, has been transformed into a society that is more about forgetting than learning, more about consuming than producing, more about asserting private interests than democratic rights. In a society obsessed with customer satisfaction and the rapid disposability of both consumer goods and long-term attachments, U.S. youth are not encouraged to participate in politics. Nor are they offered the help, guidance, and modes of education that cultivate the capacities for critical thinking and engaged citizenship. As Zygmunt Bauman points out, in a consumerist society, "the tyranny of the moment makes it difficult to live in the present, never mind understand society within a range of larger totalities."[47] Under such circumstances, according to Theodor Adorno, thinking loses its ability to point beyond itself and is reduced to mimicking existing certainties and modes of common sense. In this case, thought cannot sustain itself and becomes short-lived, fickle, and ephemeral. The late Frankfurt School theorist, Leo Lowenthal, goes further and argues that under modern systems of terror, "Thinking becomes a stupid crime; it endangers his life. The inevitable consequence is that stupidity spreads as a contagious disease among the terrorized population. Human beings live in a state of stupor, in a moral coma."[48]

If young people do not display a strong commitment to democratic politics and collective struggle, it is because they have lived through thirty years of "a debilitating and humiliating disinvestment in their future," especially if they are marginalized by class, ethnicity, and race.[49] What is new about this generation of young people is that they have experienced firsthand the relentless spread of a neoliberal pedagogical apparatus, with its celebration of an unbridled individualism and its near pathological disdain for community, public values, and the public good. They have been inundated by a market-driven value system that encourages a culture of competitiveness and produces a theater of cruelty that has resulted in "a weakening of democratic pressures, a growing inability to act politically, [and] a massive exit from politics and from responsible citizenship."[50] If U.S. students are not protesting in large numbers the ongoing intense attack on higher education and the welfare state, it might be because they have been born into a society that is tantamount to what Alex Honneth has called "an abyss of failed sociality [one in which] their perceived suffering has still not found resonance in the public space of articulation."[51]

Of course, there are students in the United States who are involved in protesting the great injustices they see around them, including the wars in Afghanistan and Iraq, the corruption of U.S. politics by casino capitalism, a permanent war economy, and the growing disinvestment in public and higher education. But they are indeed a minority, and not because they are part of what is often called a "failed generation."[52] On the contrary, the failure lies elsewhere and points to the psychological and social consequences of growing up under a neoliberal regime that goes to great lengths to privatize hope, derail public values, and undercut political commitments. The way society conceptualizes youth, especially poor youth of color, has changed from viewing youth as a symbol of hope and promise to seeing them as a sign of trouble and threat. What is clear as a result of this "failed sociality" is that if democracy is going to deliver on its promises, not only do young people need to have a passion for public values, social responsibility, and participation in society, but they also need access to those public spaces that guarantee the rights of free speech, dissent, a quality education, and critical dialogue.

Worth repeating is the notion that at the heart of such public spaces is a formative culture that creates citizens who are critical thinkers capable of making power accountable, dialogue possible, and politics a matter of shared responsibility so that democracy becomes "a new type of regime in the full sense of the term."[53] Young people need to be educated both as a condition of autonomy and for the sustainability of democratization as an ongoing movement. Not only does a substantive democracy demand citizens capable of self- and social criticism, but it also, once again, requires a critical formative culture in which people are provided with the knowledge and skills to be able to participate in such a society. What we see in the struggle for educational reforms in Europe and the Middle East is a larger struggle for the economic, political, and social conditions that give meaning and substance to what it means to make democracy possible. When we see fifteen-year-olds battle the established oppressive orders in the streets of Paris, Cairo, London, Damascus, and Athens for a more just society, they offer a glimpse of what it means for youth to enter "modernist narratives as trouble."[54] But *trouble* here exceeds dominant society's eagerness to view them as pathological, as monsters, and a drain on the market-driven order. Instead, trouble speaks to something more suggestive of a "productive unsettling of dominant epistemic regimes under the heat of desire, frustration, or anger."[55] The expectations that frame market-driven societies are losing their grip on young people who can no longer be completely seduced or controlled by the tawdry promises and failed returns of corporate-dominated and authoritarian regimes.

These youth movements tell us that the social visions embedded in casino capitalism and deeply authoritarian regimes have lost their utopian thrust and their ability to persuade and intimidate through threats, coercion, and state violence. Rejecting the terrors of the present and the modernist dreams of progress at any cost, young people have become, at least for the moment, harbingers of democracy fashioned through the desires, dreams, and hopes of a world based on the principles of equality, justice, and freedom. In doing so, they are pointing to a world order in which the future will certainly not mimic the present. What has been characterized by some commentators as an outburst of youthful utopianism reminiscent of the 1960s must in fact be seen as the outcome of "the most concrete and pressing reality."[56] Youth culture has proven to be global in its use of new media, music, and fashion and increasingly in terms of its collective anger against deep-seated injustice and its willingness to struggle against such forces. It is only a matter of time before U.S. youth recognize that they are more than consumers, market-driven society is not synonymous with democracy, private rights are not more important than the social good, and society's view of them as pathological and disposable demands a call for massive resistance in the streets, schools, and all other public spaces in which justice and democracy matter.

One of the most famous slogans of May 1968 was "Be realistic, demand the impossible." The spirit of that slogan is alive once again. But if it is to become more than a slogan, young people in the United States must join their counterparts across the globe in struggling to continue to build the formative cultures, critical public spheres, social movements, and democratic institutions necessary to make that recognition and struggle possible. Thus, once again, the most important question to be raised about U.S. students is not why they do not engage in massive protests, but when will they look beyond the norms, discourses, and rewards of the neoliberal society they have inherited from their elders? When will they begin to learn from their youthful counterparts protesting all over the globe that the first step in building a democratic society is to imagine a future different than the one that now stunts their dreams as much as their social reality? Only then can they be successful in furthering the hard and crucial task of struggling collectively to make a future based on the promise of democratic freedom happen. Taking a cue from the youth movement that helped to topple the Hosni Mubarak government, U.S. youth must have a grasp on their rights, know how to fight for them, and realize their collective power just like their counterparts in Egypt, Libya, Tunisia, Serbia, and all those other countries coming out of the darkness, heralded by the right to freedom, justice, and equality.

In what follows, I want to address the intense current assault on the social state, unions, public values, young people, democratic public spheres, such as higher education, and those other political, social, and economic forces in U.S. life that provide a counterweight against the power of mega-corporations, the rich, and the unscrupulous. In order to protect the interests of the wealthy and powerful corporations, the formative culture, social formations, and institutions necessary for a viable democracy are under an intense and wide-ranging assault. The intensity and barbarism of such an assault are evident in the current right-wing attempts to dismantle crucial social safety nets, collective-bargaining rights, unions, and the regulatory constraints on powerful corporations. This conservative assault is not just about the enactment of reactionary government policies. It is also about the proliferation of a culture of cruelty whose collateral damage is harsh and brutalizing, especially for young people and other individuals and groups marginalized by class, race, and age who now bear the burden of the worst economic recession since the 1920s. Cruelty in this instance is not meant simply to refer to the character flaws of the rich or to appeal to a form of left moralism, but to register the effects especially since the 1970s of how the institutions of capital, wealth, and power merge, not only to generate vast modes of inequality but also to inflict immense amounts of pain and suffering upon the lives of the poor, working people, the middle class, the elderly, immigrants, and young people.[57] But there is more at stake than an increase in the hard currency of human suffering. There are also disturbing signs that U.S. society is moving toward an authoritarian state largely controlled by corporations and a financial elite.[58]

Political power is now up for sale, just as government resources are increasingly being contracted out or sold off to the highest bidder. Like lemmings in heat, thousands of corporate lobbyists flock to Washington determined to corrupt the political process, while multibillionaires like the Koch brothers use their $42 billion war chest to fund right-wing think tanks, the Tea Party, and other conservative groups in order to crush the labor movement and enact legislative policies designed to decimate the social state and hand over the levers of political and economic sovereignty to the rich. Commenting on the real agenda of the Koch brothers and the Republican Party, *New York Times* op-ed writer Frank Rich rightly argues that "[t]he real goal is to reward the G.O.P.'s wealthiest patrons by crippling what remains of organized labor, by wrecking the government agencies charged with regulating and policing corporations, and, as always, by rewarding the wealthiest with more tax breaks."[59]

As the public spaces for cultivating democratic values, critical citizens, and compassionate social relations disappear, U.S. society gives rise to an army of anti-public intellectuals, a center-right media and cultural apparatus, and a damaged system of public and higher education, all of which largely function to undermine dialogue, dissent, and critical thinking in U.S. life. As politics is rewritten as a script to serve the rich and powerful, the democratic elements of social life are emptied out, smothered by an ongoing and well-financed conservative campaign to further sabotage those public spheres that enable a culture of questioning and modes of collective struggle to develop. This ideological and political assault is matched by the savagery of policies that not only amplify a growing gap between the rich and poor but also take a deadly toll on the most crucial of public services and those marginalized populations who bear the human cost of the disappearance of such services. Senator Bernie Sanders highlights some of these cuts while rightfully criticizing a federal budget that rewards millionaires and billionaires while slashing more than $60 billion from programs, which will have a deadly impact on many Americans. He enumerates some of the cuts as follows: "$1.1 billion from Head Start depriving services for 218,000 children; $1.3 billion for Social Security delaying benefits for 500,000 Americans; slash[ing] $1.3 billion from community health centers taking primary health care from 11 million patients; Pell Grants for 9.4 million low-income college students; $403 million from Community Services Block Grants affect[ing] 20 million seniors, families with children and the disabled; [and] job training and other employment services for 8 million Americans."[60] These figures are troubling and point to an exemplary register of politics that prides itself on toughness, the merits of individual responsibility, and a mode of governance in which social problems are increasingly criminalized, while those who experience such problems are left adrift to solve them on their own, regardless of whether they had any control over causing such problems in the first place. Politics has now become an extension of war and the call to austerity, a metaphor for a politics of disposability. With the collapse of the social state, those citizens viewed as disposable are now subject to a form of necropolitics, in which the social contract, however inadequate, is viewed as a drain on government resources and any notion of social protection is viewed as a pathological form of dependence.

As I have mentioned previously, complaints by right-wing politicians and conservative pundits about the growing federal deficit and their call for a harsh politics of austerity are both hypocritical and disingenuous: Hypocritical, given their support for massive tax breaks for the rich, and disingenuous, given their blatantly transparent goal of implementing a market-based agenda that imposes the burden of decreased government services and benefits on the backs of young people, the unemployed, the working class, and middle-class individuals and families. As Richard Wolff's quote suggested earlier, in this scenario, austerity measures apply to the poor but not to the rich, who continue to thrive under policies that produce government bailouts, support deficit-generating wars, tax breaks for the wealthy, and deregulation that benefits powerful corporations. The conservative and right-wing politicians and policy wonks calling for shared sacrifices made in the name of balancing budgets have no interest in promoting justice, equality, and the public good. Their policies maximize self-interest, support a culture of organized irresponsibility, and expand the pathologies of inequality, military spending, and poverty. Austerity porn functions within the current political climate to promote deficits in order to return the United States to the Gilded Age policies of the 1920s.[61]

Clearly, there is much more at stake in the current war against democracy than the reactionary ideological assertion that shared sacrifices have to be made in the name of balancing budgets. In a socioeconomic climate marked by deep economic and social inequalities, the call for shared sacrifices and responsibilities translates into the hollowing out of social services, public spheres, and educational resources that are vital to a democracy. Austerity in this script translates into an agenda that combines punishing policies with the elimination of the formative cultures and safety nets that make a decent life and political culture possible. We get a glimpse of this in Bob Herbert's rendering of the effects of such policies:

> In the real world, schools and libraries are being closed and other educational services are being curtailed. Police officers are being fired. Access to health services for poor families is being restricted. [As the Center on Budget and Policy Priorities tells us:] "At least 29 states and the District of Columbia are cutting medical, rehabilitative, home care, or other services needed by low-income people who are elderly or have disabilities, or are significantly increasing the cost of these services." ... At least 44 states and the District of Columbia have reduced overall wages paid to state workers by laying

off workers, requiring them to take unpaid leave (furloughs), freezing new hires, or similar actions. State and local governments have eliminated 407,000 jobs since August 2008, federal data show.[62]

Increasingly the unthinkable emerges in U.S. life, as market-driven policies are transformed into a specifically deadly way of exercising modes of sovereignty and government power. Budget cuts are unleashing a torrent of suffering and hardship upon more and more Americans: Poor families are being denied food stamps; conditions are being created in which houses burn down and are gutted because fire protections are now provided only for those who have paid subscriptions; prisons are being outsourced to private corporations to save money for states; thousands of people are allowed to die unnecessarily because they cannot afford health insurance; and with the banging of a legislative gavel, rights that public servants and workers have fought for over the course of many years are erased. Democracy has become a ritual controlled by a small number of extremely wealthy individuals and corporate power mongers. And, yet, as the corporate and right-wing political stranglehold is tightened around the necks of the elderly, workers, young people, and those marginalized by class and race, coalitions and the seeds of new social movements are taking shape across the United States and beginning to fight back.

Workers, students, the elderly, and young people are demonstrating in large numbers in Ohio, Wisconsin, Georgia, Montana, Tennessee, and other states against the assaults being waged on unions, public servants, and the social state in the name of concentrated corporate and political power.[63] People are now interacting with new technologies to produce shared spaces for organized struggles. Increasingly, citizens are producing counter narratives and counter-public spheres to offset the tidal wave of propaganda that informs both the liberal and right-wing media industries. The discourse of decline and cynicism has taken a hit as protest movements are emerging that are taking a cue from the drive for democracy waged by young people and workers in Egypt, Libya, Syria, France, England, Greece, and other countries that are fighting the barbarism of casino capitalism and authoritarianism's disdain for civic discourse, public values, and democratic ideals and social relations.

All of the chapters in this book take up the different elements of the current assault on the social state, workers, young people, education, and others who now occupy the liminal space of disposability. It is important to make official power visible, especially in terms of the toll it takes on those who are viewed as excess and unworthy of government supports and often excluded from the benefits of a good life. At the same time, it is important to recognize that power is not entirely subsumed within a politics of domination and that there is a growing and increasingly collective resistance to the assaults being waged on those marginalized by class, race, age, and ethnicity. The major theme that permeates this book is that if democracy is to be reclaimed as a radical idea—"the idea that people can control the functioning of society [and that] people should make decisions about all the issues that affect them"—it is crucial for progressives and others to struggle to create those formative cultures that enable people to translate private injustices into social and systemic problems.[64] Radical democracy embraces the assumption that political and individual rights are drastically limited without both economic rights and the formative cultures that make informed critical citizens possible. At stake here is a notion of democracy that refuses to be reduced to the dictates of a market society or the empty spectacle of elections controlled and paid for by corporations and wealthy elites. Such a view is crucial for those emergent social movements and struggles that suggest that democracy is once again being viewed as the "sharing of an existence that makes the political possible."[65]

In concluding, I don't want to suggest that because neoliberal and other conservative social formations appear to be winning in the United States that the struggle is over. I think it is too easy to slide from an analysis of such dominant forces to erasing the important issue that this is a struggle, however uneven, that operates within a number of different contexts and is ongoing. As Larry Grossberg has pointed out, "The fact that one can read for example a culture of cruelty off of various articulations does not yet mean that this is how people live their lives. The fact that the cultural discourses are all about markets does not mean that people live their lives with markets as the only definition/locus of value."[66] These new social formations take place within and across diverse contexts, and we need a new language for describing the nature and complexity of such forces and the diverse terrains on which they operate. I am arguing that analyzing the current political and economic assaults on democracy in the United States does not mean that an antidemocratic social formation is an accomplished and sutured fact of domination, thereby making it easier to refuse to locate it within complex and ongoing spheres of struggle.

All of the chapters in this book make clear that the dynamics of collective resistance informed by a politics of hope have to address the current crisis of public values, the eclipse of a democratic public sphere, and the disappearance of the social state. If the principles of democracy are not to be turned against themselves in order to further the savage assaults waged on the U.S. people by advocates of casino capitalism, then it is crucial to also emphasize what the late Tony Judt called the raising of social questions through a language that stresses the importance of public goods and shared responsibilities, along with a language that connects private troubles with social considerations.[67] This book, it is hoped, is a narrative of critique, recovery, and possibility, one that attempts to recast the public conversation in terms of memory as a condition for learning, higher education as a crucial public good, academics as public intellectuals, critical agency as a basis for social responsibility, and democracy as the radical frame through which meaningful political struggle becomes possible once again.

Notes

1. James Baldwin, *The Fire Next Time* (New York: Vintage, 1992), 104.

2. Elias Holtz, "The Global Student Revolt: Youth Protests Demand Education for All, Not Just for the Rich," *Socialism.com*, February 2011, online at www.socialism.com/drupal-6.8/?q=node/1568.

3. Cited in Rachel Donadio, "Europe's Young Grow Agitated over Future Prospects," *New York Times*, January 1, 2011, A6.

4. Pascale Anne Brault and Michael Naas, "Translator's Note," in Jean-Luc Nancy, *The Truth of Democracy* (New York: Fordham University Press, 2010), xi.

5. For one of the intellectual resources used by youth leaders to develop nonviolent modes of protest, see Gene Sharp, *From*

Dictatorship to Democracy (Boston: The Albert Einstein Institute, 2010), online at http://www.aeinstein.org/organizations/org/FDTD.pdf.

6. See, for instance, David D. Kirkpatrick and David E. Sanger, "Dual Uprisings Show Potent New Threats to Arab States," *New York Times,* February 13, 2011, A1.

7. John Pilger, "The Revolt in Egypt Is Coming Home," *Truthout .org,* February 10, 2011, online at http://www.truth-out.org/the-revolt-egypt-is-coming-home67624.

8. Simeon Talley, "Why Aren't Students in the U.S. Protesting Tuition, Too?" *Campus Progress,* December 23, 2010, online at http://www.campusprogress.org/articles/why_arent_students_in_the_u.s._protesting_tuition_too.

9. Cited in Donadio, "Europe's Young," A6.

10. Joao Biehl, *Vita: Life in a Zone of Social Abandonment* (Los Angeles: University of California Press, 2005).

11. John and Jean Comaroff, "Reflections on Youth, from the Past to the Postcolony," in Melissa S. Fisher and Greg Downey, eds., *Frontiers of Capital: Ethnographic Reflections on the New Economy* (Durham, NC: Duke University Press, 2006), 268.

12. Zygmunt Bauman, "Freudian Civilization Revisited—Or Whatever Happened to the Reality Principle?" *Journal of Anthropological Psychology* 21 (2009): 8.

13. Eliaz Holtz, "The Global Student Revolt." *Freedom Socialist,* February 2011, online at http://www.socialism.com/drupal-6.8/?q=node/1568.

14. Amanda Terkel, "Maine GOP Legislators Looking to Loosen Child Labor Laws," *Huffington Post,* March 30, 2011, online at http://www.huffingtonpost.com/2011/03/30/maine-gop-legislators-loo_n_842563.html.

15. Deborah Weinstein, "Paving the Road to a Hungrier, Unhealthier, and Less-Educated Nation," *CommonDreams.org,* June 21, 2011, online at http://www.commondreams.org/view/2011/06/21-0.

16. Abby Zimet, "On Ass-Backward Priorities: The Recession Is the Fault of Foster Children and Their Hoity Toity Clothes," *CommonDreams.org,* April 29, 2011, online at http://www.commondreams.org/further/2011/04/25-0.

17. I am paraphrasing here from Sally Davison, "Ecowars," *Soundings,* Issue 34, Autumn 2006, online at http://www.lwbooks.co.uk/journals/soundings/archive/editorial34.html.

18. Lawrence Grossberg, *Caught in the Crossfire: Kids, Politics, and America's Future* (Boulder, CO: Paradigm Publishers, 2005), 264.

19. Gesa Helms, Marina Vishmidt, and Lauren Berlant, "Affect and the Politics of Austerity: An Interview Exchange with Lauren

Berlant," *Variant* 39/40, Winter 2010, online at http://www
.variant.org.uk/39_40texts/Variant39_40.html#L1.

20. Richard D. Wolff, "Austerity: Why and for Whom?" *In These Times,* July 15, 2010, online at http://www.inthesetimes.com/article/6232/austerity_why_and_for_whom/.

21. Rania Khalek, "Death by Budget Cut: Why Conservatives and Some Dems Have Blood on Their Hands," *AlterNet,* June 13, 2011, online at http://www.alternet.org/story/151275/death_by_budget_cut:_why_conservatives_and_some_dems_have_blood_on_their_hands/.

22. Ibid.

23. Leo Lowenthal, "Atomization of Man," *False Prophets: Studies in Authoritarianism* (New Brunswick, NJ: Transaction Books, 1987), 182.

24. Cited in Fulvia Carnevale and John Kelsey, "Art of the Possible: An Interview with Jacques Rancière," *Artforum,* March 2007, 260–261.

25. I take this issue up in Henry A. Giroux, "The Crisis of Public Values in the Age of the New Media," *Critical Studies in Media Communication* 28:1 (2011): 8–29.

26. Jacques Rancière, "Democracy, Republic Representation," *Constellations* 13:3 (2006): 300.

27. Eliaz Holtz, "The Global Student Revolt," *Freedom Socialist,* February 2011, online at http://www.socialism.com/drupal-6.8/?q=node/1568.

28. This theme is taken up in great detail in Courtney Martin, *Do It Anyway: A New Generation of Activists* (Boston: Beacon Press, 2010). The analysis suffers from the same sort of privilege that it critiques. It suggests that not only are privileged middle-class kids the vanguard of change for this generation, but they suffer from both a narcissistic refusal to look inward and an ego-driven sense of politics that is as narrow as it is paternalistic and missionary in focus. This critique is too simple, lacks complexity, and appears to suffer from the same problem to which it is objecting.

29. Courtney E. Martin, "Why Class Matters in Campus Activism," *The American Prospect,* December 6, 2010, online at http://www.prospect.org/cs/articles?article=why_class_matters_in_campus_activism.

30. Cited in ibid.

31. Mark Edelman Boren, *Student Resistance: A History of the Unruly Subject* (New York: Routledge, 2001), 227.

32. Talley, "Why Aren't Students."

33. See, for instance, Jeff Madrick, *Age of Greed: The Triumph of Finance and the Decline of America, 1970 to the Present* (New York: Knopf, 2011).

34. Susan Searls Giroux, *Between Race and Reason: Violence, Intellectual Responsibility and the University to Come* (Stanford, CA: Stanford University Press, 2010), 79.

35. Edelman Boren, *Student Resistance*, 228.

36. Robert Reich, "The Attack on American Education," *ReaderSupportedNews.org*, December 23, 2010, online at http://www.readersupportednews.org/opinion2/299-190/4366-the-attack-on-american-education.

37. In a personal correspondence to me, David Theo Goldberg spells out the nature of the cuts at the University of California system. He writes, "The projection for next year is a $500 million cut to the UC budget from previous state support of $3.3 billion or so (and an overall budget of $19 billion) for the system. About a $50 million cut to each of the campuses. And another $500 million unfunded mandate to pick up campus contributions to pensions. So we are looking at something like an overall 3–6 percent cut of entire budget (including salaries and student support and all). Student fees have increased a total of 40 percent in [the] past two years, though only those whose families earn more than $180,000 a year get to pay the full fees; those earning under somewhere in the vicinity of $80,000 a year pay no fees at all—so about half [of the] UC student population pay less than full fees. That said, [Governor Jerry] Brown has mandated that UC cannot raise fees again to deal with the next round of cuts—or else will lose further state funding proportionately. And where California goes often goes the rest of the nation."

38. There are many books and articles that take up this issue. One of the most incisive commentators is Jeffrey Williams, "Student Debt and the Spirit of Indenture," *Dissent*, Fall 2008, online at http://www.dissentmagazine.org/article/?article=1303.

39. David Masciotra, "The Rich Get Richer and the Young Go into Deep Debt," *BuzzFlash*, December 6, 2010, online at http://blog.buzzflash.com/node/12045.

40. Simon Head, "The Grim Threat to British Universities," *New York Review of Books*, January 13, 2011, online at http://www.nybooks.com/articles/archives/2011/jan/13/grim-threat-british-universities/.

41. Jean-Luc Nancy, *The Truth of Democracy*, trans. Pascale-Anne Brault and Michael Naas (New York: Fordham University Press, 2010), 9.

42. Tom Engelhardt, "An American World War: What to Watch for in 2010," *TruthOut.org*, January 3, 2010, online at http://www.truth-out.org/topstories/10410vh4. See also Andrew Bacevich, *The New American Militarism* (New York: Oxford University Press, 2005) and Chalmers Johnson, *Nemesis: The Last Days of the American Empire* (New York: Metropolitan Books, 2006).

43. Dave Lindorff, "The US Military's A/C Bill for Iraq and Afghanistan Gives Me the Shivers," *CounterPunch,* June 29, 2011, online at www.counterpunch.com/lindorff0629011.html.

44. Eric Gorski, "45% of Students Don't Learn Much in College," *Huffington Post,* January 21, 2011, online at http://www .huffingtonpost.com/2011/01/18/45-of-students-don't-learn_n_ 810224.html. The study is taken from Richard Arum and Josipa Roksa, *Academically Adrift: Limited Learning on College Campuses* (Chicago: University of Chicago Press, 2011).

45. An excellent analysis of the Tea Party Movement can be found in Paul Street and Anthony DiMaggio, *Crashing the Tea Party: Mass Media and the Campaign to Remake American Politics* (Boulder, CO: Paradigm Publishers, 2011). For an informative commentary on these anti-union tactics and assaults on public school teachers and public education, see Faiz Shakir, Benjamin Armbruster, George Zornick, Zaid Jilani, Alex Seitz-Wald, and Tanya Somanader, "The Main Street Movement," *The Progress Report,* February 23, 2011, online at http://pr.thinkprogress.org/2011/02/pr20110223/. For those who believe that public workers are the problem, this chart on inequality tells a different story altogether. See Dave Gilson and Carolyn Perot, "It's the Inequality, Stupid," *Mother Jones,* March/ April 2011, online at http://motherjones.com/politics/2011/02/ income-inequality-in-america-chart-graph.

46. Sheldon S. Wolin, *Democracy Incorporated: Managed Democracy and the Specter of Inverted Totalitarianism* (Princeton, NJ: Princeton University Press, 2008), 259–260.

47. Zygmunt Bauman, *Does Ethics Have a Chance in a World of Consumers?* (Cambridge, MA: Harvard University Press, 2008), 159.

48. Leo Lowenthal, "Atomization of Man," *False Prophets: Studies in Authoritarianism* (New Brunswick, NJ: Transaction Books, 1987), 182.

49. Ibid., 235. I have also taken up this theme in great detail in Henry A. Giroux, *Youth in a Suspect Society* (New York: Palgrave Macmillan, 2010).

50. Zygmunt Bauman, *The Individualized Society* (London: Polity, 2001), 55.

51. Alex Honneth, *Pathologies of Reason* (New York: Columbia University Press, 2009), 188.

52. Surely, there is a certain irony in the fact that the work of Gene Sharp, a little-known U.S. theorist in nonviolent action, is inspiring young people all over the world to resist authoritarian governments. Yet, his work is almost completely ignored by young people in the United States. See, for instance, Sheryl Gay Stolberg, "Shy U.S. Intellectual Created Playbook Used in Revolution," *New*

York Times, February 16, 2011, A1. See, in particular, Sharp, *From Dictatorship to Democracy.*

53. Cornelius Castoriadis, "Democracy as Procedure and Democracy as Regime," *Constellations* 4:1 (1997): 10.

54. John and Jean Comaroff, "Reflections of Youth," 268.

55. Ibid.

56. Cited in Brault and Naas, "Translators Note," xii.

57. This issue is taken up in great detail in Zygmunt Bauman, *Collateral Damage: Social Inequalities in a Global Age* (London: Polity Press, 2011).

58. There are too many books on this issue to list them all. Some of the more notable are Sheldon S. Wolin, *Democracy Incorporated: Managed Democracy and the Specter of Inverted Totalitarianism* (Princeton, NJ: Princeton University Press, 2008); Henry A. Giroux, *Against the Terror of Neoliberalism* (Boulder, CO: Paradigm Publishers, 2008); Chris Hedges, *Death of the Liberal Class* (Toronto: Knopf Canada, 2010); and Jacob S. Hacker and Paul Pierson, *Winner-Take-All Politics* (New York: Simon and Schuster, 2010).

59. Frank Rich, "Why Wouldn't the Tea Party Shut It Down?," *New York Times,* February 24, 2011, WK8. See Jane Mayer, "Covert Operations: The Billionaire Brothers Who Are Waging a War Against Obama," *The New Yorker,* August 30, 2010, online at http://www.newyorker.com/reporting/2010/08/30/100830fa_fact_mayer.

60. Bernie Sanders cited in editorial, "Bernie Sanders: Don't Balance the Budget on the Backs of the Middle Class," *BuzzFlash.com,* March 2, 2011, online at http://blog.buzzflash.com/node/12430.

61. James Crotty, "High Deficits Were the Objective of Right Economics," *The Real News,* May 10, 2011, online at http://therealnews.com/t2/index.php?option=com_content&task=view&id=31&Itemid=74&jumival=6724.

62. Bob Herbert, "A Terrible Divide," *New York Times,* February 7, 2011, A27.

63. Zaid Jilani, "Main Street Movement Erupts as Thousands Across Country Protest War on the Middle Class," *Think Progress Report,* February 24, 2011, online at http://mycommonsensepolitics.net/index.php?option=com_content&view=article&id=2711:main-street-movement-erupts-as-thousands-across-country-protest-war-on-the-middle-class&catid=27:tree-of-liberty&Itemid=134.

64. Ian Angus, *Emergent Publics: An Essay on Social Movements and Democracy* (Winnipeg, MA: Arbeiter Ring Publishing, 2001), 34.

65. Brault and Naas, "Translator's Note," xi.

66. Lawrence Grossberg, Personal Correspondence, June 18, 2011.

67. Tony Judt, *Ill Fares the Land* (New York: The Penguin Press, 2010).

◆

1

In the Twilight of the Social State

Rethinking Walter Benjamin's Angel of History[1]

> By eviscerating public services and reducing them to a
> network of farmed-out private providers, we have begun to
> dismantle the fabric of the state. As for the dust and powder
> of individuality: it resembles nothing so much as Hobbes's
> war of all against all, in which life for many people has once
> again become solitary, poor and more than a little nasty.
> —*Tony Judt*[2]

Responding in 1940 to the unfolding catastrophes perpe-
trated by the rise of fascism in Germany, Walter Benjamin,
a German Jewish philosopher and literary critic, wrote his
now famous "Theses on the Philosophy of History." In the
Ninth Thesis, Benjamin comments on Paul Klee's painting
Angelus Novus:

> "Angelus Novus" shows an angel looking as though he is
> about to move away from something he is fixedly contem-
> plating. His eyes are staring, his mouth is open, his wings
> are spread. This is how one pictures the angel of history. His
> face is turned toward the past. Where we perceive a chain
> of events, he sees one single catastrophe which keeps piling
> wreckage upon wreckage and hurls it in front of his feet.
> The Angel would like to stay, awaken the dead, and make
> whole what has been smashed. But a storm is blowing from

Paradise; it has got caught in his wings with such violence that the angel can no longer close them. The storm irresistibly propels into the future to which his back is turned, while the pile of debris before him grows skyward. This storm is what we call progress.[3]

The meaning and significance of Benjamin's angel of history has been the subject of varied interpretations by philosophers, literary critics, and others.[4] Yet, it still offers us a powerful lesson about a set of historical conditions marked by a "catastrophe that keeps piling wreckage upon wreckage."[5] In this instance, catastrophe both undermined any hope of democracy in Europe and gave rise to the dark forces of a brutal authoritarianism and the cool, ruthless homage to efficiency and the industrialization of death. In the midst of such a crisis, Benjamin's angel is frozen in time, paralyzed by a storm called "progress" that pulls him into the future without being able to "awaken the dead" or mend the catastrophe at his feet.

For Benjamin, the storm of progress was a mode of modernity gone askew and a deceit that made a claim on happiness rather than the horrors of destruction, constituting a set of conditions that unleashed a barrage of unimaginable carnage and suffering in the 1930s and 1940s. The utopian belief in technologically assisted social improvement had given way to a dystopian project of mad violence that would inevitably produce the context for Benjamin to take his own life in 1940. According to Benjamin, the horrors of the past made it difficult to believe in progress as a narrative of the advancement of human civilization. In fact, as Zygmunt Bauman has pointed out, it wasn't just the overdetermined force of history that was at stake in Benjamin's narrative, but also the notion that "we are pulled forward by future happiness—[when] in fact, [as Benjamin noted], we are pushed from behind by the horror of destruction we keep perpetrating on the way."[6] Undoubtedly, Benjamin's angel of history would be at home today. And, yet, even in the darkest times, there were people brave enough to struggle for a more open-ended understanding of history and a more promising democratic future, waging that the catastrophes of the past and the false claims of a history propelled by predetermined laws and order-building imperatives could be prevented through a kind of memory work and politics in which such atrocities were acknowledged and condemned as part of a larger project of freedom, collective struggle, and social justice.

Like the angel of history in Benjamin's rendering of Klee's painting, the U.S. public is surrounded by another catastrophe of history, inconceivable but manifest in the horrible suffering produced by two unnecessary wars in Iraq and Afghanistan, and the current economic recession, exacerbating already high levels of poverty, homelessness, and joblessness now spreading like a poisonous blight across the U.S. landscape. But unlike the forces constricting Benjamin's angel, the storm that pins the wings of the current diminutive angel of history is more intense, more paralyzing in its hyper-materialistic visions, and more privatizing in its definition of agency. The historical forces producing this storm and its accompanying catastrophes are incorrigibly blind to the emergence of a "pulverized, atomized society spattered with the debris of broken inter-human bonds and their eminently frail and breakable substitutes."[7] This is best exemplified in the now infamous and cruel tenets of a harsh neoliberalism stated without apology by Ronald Reagan and Margaret Thatcher in the 1980s, including the claims that "government is the problem not the solution" and "there is no such thing as society."

Social progress has ceded the historical stage to individual actions, values, tastes, and personal success, just as any notion of the common and public good that once defined the meaning of progress is rendered as a pathology, the vestige of a kind of socialist nightmare that squelches any possibility of individual freedom and responsibility. If progress even in its mythic register was once associated, however flawed, with lifting the populace from the bondage of necessity, suffering, and exploitation, today it has been stripped of any residual commitment to the collective good and functions largely as a kind of nostalgic relic of a historical period in U.S. history, in which a concept of the *social state* "was not always a term of opprobrium" or a metaphor for state terrorism.[8] The language of progress, however false, has been replaced by the discourse and politics of austerity—which is neoliberal code for making the working and middle classes bear the burden of a financial crisis caused by hedge fund operators, banking and investment houses, and the mega-rich.[9]

The catastrophe that marks the current historical moment no longer wraps itself in the mantle of progress. On the contrary, the storm brewing in the United States and other parts of the globe represent a kind of anti-progress, a refusal to think about, invest in, or address the shared responsibilities that come with a viable vision of the future and "the good society." Composing meaningful visions of the good society that benefit citizens in general rather than a select few is now viewed as "a waste of time, since they are irrelevant to individual happiness and a successful life."[10] Bounded by the narrow, private worlds that make up their everyday lives, the U.S. public has surrendered to the atomizing consequences of a market-driven morality and society and has replaced the call for communal responsibility with the call to further one's own interests at all costs. The social and its most significant embodiment—the welfare state—is now viewed as an albatross around the neck of neoliberal notions of accumulation (as opposed to "progress"). Society has become hyper-individualized, trapped by the lure of material success and stripped of any obligation to the other. Zygmunt Bauman argues that in such a society,

> individual men and women are now expected, pushed and pulled to seek and find individual solutions to socially created problems and implement those solutions individually using individual skills and resources. This ideology proclaims the futility (indeed, counter productivity) of solidarity: of joining forces and subordinating individual actions to a "common cause." It derides the principle of communal responsibility for the well-being of its members, decrying it as a recipe for a debilitating "nanny state," and warning against care for the other leading to an abhorrent and detestable "dependency."[11]

Our contemporary angel of history has been transformed into a "swarm of angels of biographies—a crowd of loners"[12] whose wings are stuck in a storm propelled by the hatred of democracy and a contempt for any claim on the future in which the state functions to offer even a modicum of social protection. And although Benjamin's angel of history rightfully disputes the false claims of an order building progress, he has been replaced by a multitude of privatizing corporate-beholden angels who cede any notion of society and collective vision—reduced to wingless messengers trapped in their own biographies and individual experiences, cut off from any viable notion of society and its fundamental social solidarities. At the same time, the storm that pins the wings of the contemporary angels of history is fueled by an intense disdain for the social state, which Bauman describes in the following manner:

> A state is "social" when it promotes the principle of *communally endorsed*, collective insurance against individual misfortune and its consequences. It is primarily that principle—declared, set in operation and trusted to be in working order—that recast the otherwise abstract idea of "society" into the experience of felt and lived community through replacing the "order of egoism" (to deploy John Dunn's terms), bound to generate an atmosphere of mutual mistrust and suspicion, with the "order of equality," inspiring confidence and solidarity. It is the same principle which lifts members of society to the status of *citizens*, that is, makes them stakeholders in addition to being stockholders: beneficiaries, but also actors—the wardens as much as the wards of the "social benefits" system, individuals with an acute interest in the common good understood as a network of shared institutions that can be trusted, and realistically expected, to guarantee the solidity and reliability of the state-issued "collective insurance policy."[13]

We no longer live in an age in which history's "winged messengers" bear witness to the suffering endured by millions and the conditions that allow such suffering to continue. Thinking about past and future has collapsed into a presentism in which the delete button, the utter normalization of a punishing inequality, and the atomizing pleasures of instant gratification come together to erase any notion of historical consciousness and any vestige of social and moral responsibility owed as much to future generations as to the dead. The "winged messengers" have been replaced by a less hallowed breed of anti-public intellectuals, academics, journalists, and artists, who now cater to the demands of the market and further their careers by becoming cheerleaders for neoliberal capitalism. The legacies now left by too many intellectuals have more to do with establishing a corporate friendly brand name than fighting economic and social injustices, translating private into public issues, or creating genuine public spheres that promote critical thought and collective action. Whatever "winged messengers" do exist are either banished to the margins of the institutions that house them or excluded by the dominant media that have now become a mouthpiece for corporate culture and the new global rich.

As history is erased and economics becomes the driving force for all aspects of political, cultural, and social life, those institutional and political forces that hold the reins of power now become the purveyors of social death, comfortably ensconced in a political imaginary that wreaks human misery on the planet as the rich and powerful reap huge financial gains for themselves. The principal players of casino capitalism live in the highly circumscribed time of short-term investments and financial gains and they are more than willing to close their eyes to the carnage and suffering all around them while they are sucked into the black hole of the future. As the social state is eviscerated by an all-embracing market fundamentalism, society increasingly becomes a machine for destroying the power of civic culture and civic life, proliferating the ideologies and technologies of what is increasingly and unequivocally becoming a punishing state. And, paraphrasing Achille Mbembe, politics becomes a form of social death in which "the future is collapsed into the present."[14]

Though helpless to control what he saw, Benjamin's angel of history recognized that the past, present, and future were inextricably linked in a constellation of ideas, events, social practices, and relations of power that mutually inform each other. History offered no guarantees, and although it could often paralyze and punish, the potentially revolutionary ideal that gave it mythic status was organized around an understanding of social improvement that was partly connected to the unfinished business of human possibility and betterment. Of course, Benjamin rejected such a view. His angel of history is caught up in a storm that paralyzed human agency while putting the myth of the inevitability of progress to rest. But storms pass, and hope as a condition for conceptualizing a future of sustainable progress can offer us both space and time for reflection, for developing modes of individual critique and collective agency capable of addressing and dismantling those sites of agony and wretchedness made visible in the afterglow of historical consciousness. The problems confronting Americans today are very different from what Benjamin faced in the years before his suicide in 1940, but they share with the past a dangerous and threatening element of authoritarianism evident in the force and power of their ability to eliminate from public discussion what Tony Judt has called the social question and what I have referred to as the punishing state.[15]

In an age when personal and political rights are undermined by a lack of economic rights, the utter reliance on a stripped-down notion of individual freedom and choice, coupled with a strong emphasis on personal responsibility, turns people away from those larger forces that nonetheless determine (but do not overdetermine) their varied daily experiences. Moreover, the ongoing privatization, commodification, militarization, and deregulation that now shape U.S. society produce a range of crises and problems that extend far beyond the reach of the isolated and atomized individual. Within this dystopian, neoliberal economic order, "the language of rights has changed: *citizens* have become 'customers'; passengers and hospital patients have become 'clients'; *poverty* has become criminalized and 'extreme poverty' has become a 'pathological condition' rather than a reflection of structural injustice—a 'pathological dysfunction' of those who are poor, rather than the structural dysfunction of an economic system that generates and reproduces inequality."[16] How else to explain the increasing numbers of people being thrown into jail because they have failed to pay their debts or young people being booked and imprisoned because they violated a trivial rule such as breaking a school dress code?[17] But there is more at work here than a society without social protections. There is also a cruel and deadly ideology of privatization and punishment in which the importance of the social responsibility, public goods, and public values is completely erased from a language derived from ideas based in marketing, commodification, and brand loyalty.

As the United States moves, in Bauman's terms, from a society of producers to a society of consumers, the state increasingly becomes an "executor of market sovereignty" and is further transformed as the much-needed protections of the social state are replaced by its policing functions.[18] If

Benjamin's angel of history were to serve, once again, as an insightful witness to the multiple catastrophes facing the United States today, it would be stuck in an equally danger-ous storm being produced by casino capitalism. But rather than looking down on such catastrophes, the angel would be blindfolded, its arms would be handcuffed behind its back, and its wings would remain paralyzed. Caught in the winds of a society in which the global corporation abandoned all to the Darwinian shark tank, the angel of history cannot bear witness to this new culture of cruelty—so ubiquitous is it that one fails to notice—nor can it alert us to the new threats facing democracy itself. On the contrary, it now symbolizes how society functions to make all elements for bearing wit-ness and hope, however problematic, fodder for the age of excess and the new politics of disposability. This is a kind of politics in which the only value that matters is the bottom line and the most revered political practice is what David Harvey calls "accumulation by dispossession"—the ruthless appropriation of the few resources that allow the downtrod-den to survive in order to augment capitalist class power.[19] The angel of history has been transformed into a symbol of death, a symbol that could only emerge from a society that no longer has any ethical consciousness and incessantly expands its politics of disposability to those elements of the population who are now regarded as failed consumers, workers, and critics.

The survival-of-the-fittest ethic and its mantra of doing just about anything to increase profits now reach into every aspect of society and are widely dispersed as a form of public pedagogy in the dominant and new media. Disposability and social death replace civic life with a culture of greed and cruel spectacles, which have become a register of how difficult it is for U.S. society to make any claims on the ideal or even promise of a democracy to come. As the realm of democratic politics shrinks and is turned over to market forces, social bonds crumble and any representation of communal cohe-sion is treated with disdain. Under the reign of casino capi-talism, freedom is stripped of its social responsibilities and moral considerations are banished from politics. As the realm of the social disappears, public values and any consideration of the common good are erased from politics, while the social state and responsible modes of governing are replaced by a punishing state. Evidence of such a transformation is apparent as social problems are increasingly criminalized; a war is waged on the poor rather than on poverty; debtor prisons reminiscent of Charles Dickens's novels emerge to torment impoverished Americans;[20] social welfare agencies are increasingly modeled after prisons; young people are more than ever being warehoused in schools that inflict dead time upon their minds and bodies; unprecedented mass racialized incarceration continues unabated; and the punishment apparatus increasingly inserts itself into every sphere of U.S. society, while derailing the project of democracy in multiple ways.[21] The rise of the punishing state merges the former functions of the welfare state with crime control, incarcerates more than 2.3 million people considered disposable factions of the working class and underprivileged, and legitimates punishment and crime control as a mode of governance and cultural practice.[22]

As shared responsibilities give way to individual fears, human suffering and hardship disappear behind the disparaging discourse of individual responsibility in which the poor, unemployed, homeless, and hungry bear the ultimate blame for their own misfortune. The neoliberal appeal to self-responsibility and the politics of shame now function as a kind of parlor magic in obliterating any trace of the larger social and systemic forces wreaking havoc on U.S. society. In this discourse of privatization, there are no public or systemic problems, only individual troubles with no trace or connection to larger social forces. Market infatuation with profits and self-interest not only erodes public values and the moral dimensions of the larger social order, but also creates the conditions for a state whose governance is now outsourced to corporate interests. And as the corporate state replaces the democratic state, however minimal it appears, there is nothing to bind ordinary citizens to the notion of democratic governance and a social state. Instead, the state becomes an object of both disdain and fear.

Rage, vengeance, fear, insecurity, and state violence increasingly give rise to a culture of cruelty, producing an ugly moral crisis that extends far beyond the walls of the prison, courts, and criminal justice system. Within the larger apparatuses of cultural representation, we are increasingly confronted by images, discourses, and signs that reveal punishment and cruelty as practices moving through the U.S. landscape and serve as both commentary and entertainment normalizing the domestic terrorism, massive human suffering, and moral irresponsibility that have come to define U.S. society. This should not be surprising in a society in which politics is entirely driven by a Darwinian corporate ideology and a militaristic mind-set that atomize the individual, celebrate the survival of the fittest, and legitimate "privatization, gross inequalities, and an obsession with wealth," regardless of the collective moral depravity and individual and social impoverishment produced by such inequities.[23]

The collapse of the social state with its state protections, public values, and democratic governance can be seen in how the Bush and Obama administrations embraced the logic of the market and farmed out government responsibilities to private contractors who undercut the power of the welfare state while waging a war on human dignity, moral compassion, social responsibility, and life itself. Everything is up for sale under this form of economic Darwinism, including prisons, schools, military forces, and the temporary faculty hired to fill the ranks of a depleted academy. Evidence of such a Darwinian ideology and militaristic mind-set is visible in the attack on working people and labor unions, the waging of two unnecessary wars, and the destruction of the nation's safety net; it is also well-illustrated in images so cruel and inhuman that they serve as flashpoints signaling not only a rupture from the ideals of democracy but also an embrace of antidemocratic tendencies that testify to an emerging authoritarianism in the United States.

One such frightening image appeared recently in the national media when, in rural Tennessee, firefighters "looked on as a house burned because the family who lived in it had not paid the $75 annual fire-protection fee. Their home was destroyed—along with three puppies that were inside."[24] The owner of the home, Gene Cranick, claimed that he had simply forgotten to pay the $75 annual fee for fire protection, and when the firefighting team finally arrived—because it threatened the surrounding homes of people who had paid the fee—he offered to pay on the spot. The firemen not only refused to accept the payment, but stood by and joked as the family pleaded for their help and the home burned to the ground.[25] Such acts of cruelty are not limited to a specific moronic group of arsonists posing as public servants. This horrendous act of moral negligence was also echoed among many conservative commentators. For example, one of the most prominent conservative television and radio hosts, Glenn Beck, defended the cruel actions of the firefighters, claiming it was necessary to prevent people from "'sponging off' their neighbors. . . . While Beck defended the firefighters, his on-air sidekick made fun of Mr. Cranick for trying to get the fire put out—and mocked his southern accent."[26] Such events seem unimaginable in a country that defines itself as a democratic society and pridefully presents to the world its legacy of "shared purpose and common institutions."[27] Even after the gross display of government irresponsibility surrounding the tragedy of Hurricane Katrina and its needless death and destruction—all of which might have served as a wake-up call—the flight from social responsibility and the demands of the ethical imagination continues. This is amply evident in the ongoing refusal on the part of the U.S. public to remember the consequences of turning state power over to corporations and privatized interests. It just might be that the cult of privatization and the worship of corporate power have not only eviscerated public services but also engulfed a large number of Americans in a kind of moral coma, allowing them and "state-run agencies [to abandon] the care and responsibility of individuals."[28]

A similar example of the neoliberal culture of cruelty was on full display when the conservative governor of Arizona, Jan Brewer, cut funding for certain organ transplants from the state's Medicaid program. Many patients who had been on a donor list for more than a year were notified by the state that they were no longer on the list and that the only way they could get a life-saving transplant would be to pay for it themselves. Transplants that had been authorized for nearly one hundred people were revoked as a cost-cutting measure. As Marc Lacey pointed out in the *New York Times*, "Many doctors say the decision amounts to a death sentence for some low-income patients, who have little chance of survival without transplants and lack the hundreds of thousands of dollars needed to pay for them."[29] Most of the people on the list are too poor to pay for the procedure, and, as such, are now victims of a law that truly made them disposable by imposing a death sentence on them. What is especially disturbing about this case is that the cuts were justified on the grounds that patients who receive certain transplants do not live very long, and yet the statistics used to justify the state legislators' decision were based on incomplete data.[30] Because of the negative national attention this shameful piece of legislation received, it was later reversed.

Neoliberalism's disdain for social protections and its embrace of a politics of disposability become even more obvious when it was reported that "the same state whose representatives filed a lawsuit challenging [Obama's] new health care law because it requires people to purchase health insurance . . . decided to cut the health insurance of heart transplant patients."[31] Advocates of neoliberal austerity measures, given their hatred of Obama's health plan, were more than willing to mandate a death sentence to the ailing poor rather than give them an option to get health insurance that might have saved their lives. It gets worse. Governor Brewer claimed the state will save $1.4 million by enacting the law (which amounts to about one-tenth of 1 percent of the state's $825 million deficit). What is truly morally reprehensible is that the same legislature that enacted Brewer's death law "decided to spend $1.2 million to 'build bridges for endangered squirrels over a mountain road so they don't become road-kill.'"[32] As one commentator put it, "Yes, they are willing to spend more than a million dollars to save five squirrels a year, but not to give someone a new heart. Now that's a heartless death panel."[33] Since the law was enacted, at least two people have died because they were denied state aid for organ transplants. The promise of a collective identity and common purpose is upended in these examples and far too many others to record here. Undoubtedly, these examples raise the question of what kind of society we have become. The question left unasked by the proponents of a ruthless neoliberal agenda but demanding an answer from the rest of us is, What kind of future do we want our children to inherit?

At a frightening speed, Americans are abandoning public values, public goods, and a sense of common purpose that are integral to the social state and that were expressed historically in the noble struggle for human rights, social services, and public provisions during Franklin Delano Roosevelt's New Deal and Lyndon Johnson's Great Society. We seem to have given up on social policies that lend protections and exhibit compassion to those crippled by the misfortune of bad health, poverty, and the lack of the most basic necessities for survival. It seems unimaginable in the current cutthroat climate to remember or once again hear President Roosevelt's call for all Americans to support an economic Bill of Rights in his fourth State of the Union address:

> We have come to a clear realization of the fact that true individual freedom cannot exist without economic security and independence. "Necessitous men are not free men." *People who are hungry and out of a job are the stuff of which dictatorships are made.* In our day these economic truths have become accepted as self-evident. We have accepted, so to speak, a second Bill of Rights under which a new basis of security and prosperity can be established for all regardless of station, race, or creed.[34] [my emphasis]

Benjamin's angel of history has now been blinded and can no longer see the destruction beneath its feet or the storm clouds paralyzing its wings. It is now stuck in a storm without a past and lacking any consideration of the future. Concern with the social good has been replaced by an obsessive investment in individualism, a shared sense of purpose has been beseiged by combative relations; and a desire to prevent injustice has been superseded by a desire for instant fame and the sordid glamor of celebrity culture. The current age of precariousness has been downsized in importance, as the new Gilded Age and those it privileges take center stage. The task of continually creating a democracy has been replaced by the struggle to endlessly produce new markets that offer the promise of nearly unimaginable financial gain. As Zygmunt Bauman points out, morality has become painless, "stripped of obligations and executive sanctions, 'adapted to the Ego-priority.'"[35] Under such circumstances, democratic politics, if not politics itself, is held hostage to the rapacious greed of the ultrarich and megacorporations, as inequality in wealth and income spread through the country like a raging wildfire.

As we move into the second Gilded Age, with its reproduction of massive inequalities and a life of privilege for the few, we are confronted with a level of suffering that is unprecedented. Although the following statistics cannot portray the level of existential pain caused by the inequalities that produce so much unnecessary suffering, they do provide snapshots of those structural forces and institutions that increasingly make life difficult for millions of Americans under a ruthless form of economic Darwinism. Such statistics also bring home the importance of going beyond just criticizing in the abstract the values and rationality that drive neoliberal market fundamentalism. As Slavoj Žižek has rightly pointed out, when it comes to the neoliberal-driven crisis, the social and economic problem that must be addressed forcefully is the growing gap and antagonism between the included and the excluded.[36] And this gap must not only be made visible, it must be confronted with pedagogical care around the question of whether democracy is still an appropriate name for the United States' political system, given the gulf, if not chasm, between the rich and the poor, the privileged and the underprivileged.[37]

One measure of how the economic elite is destroying the United States and waging a war on the poor, working class, and middle class can be seen in the fact that despite being one of the richest countries in the world, the United States has the highest poverty rate in industrialized world. More than 44 million people, or one in seven Americans, live below the poverty line.[38] In recent years, the steepest rise in poverty has taken place among children, with some experts predicting that 6 million kids will be living in poverty in the next decade.[39] In addition, more than 50 million people cannot eat without food stamps, and a stunning 50 percent of U.S. children will use food stamps to eat at some point in their childhood. Regarding health insurance, a staggering 50 million Americans have none, a figure that becomes even more disturbing when a runaway unemployment rate of 20 percent is factored into the equation. If we count all the "uncounted workers—'involuntary part-time' and 'discouraged workers'—the unemployment rate rises from 9.7 percent to over 20 percent."[40] On top of this, we have 3 million people who are homeless, and more than 5 million who have lost their homes; by 2014, it has been predicted that this last figure will rise to 13 million. The standard of living for the average American plummeted during the economic crisis— "the median American household net worth was $102,500 in 2007, and went down to $65,400 in 2009."[41] Meanwhile, against such staggering poverty, loss, human despair, and massive inequality in wealth and income, the top 1 percent of the population has massively increased its wealth and power. For instance, Matt Taibbi claims that the top 1 percent has seen its share of the nation's overall wealth jump from 34.6 percent before the crisis in 2007 to more than 37.1 percent in 2009. The top corporate executives collect a salary that gives them $500 for every $1 earned by the average worker. The wages of the 75 wealthiest Americans "increased from $91.2 million in 2008 to an astonishing $518.8 million in 2009. That's nearly $10 million in weekly pay!"[42] As Robert Reich points out, "The top one-tenth of 1 percent of Americans now earn as much as the bottom 120 million of us."[43] In addition, the top 1 percent owns 70 percent of all financial assets, an all-time record. In light of these trends, it is hardly surprising to read that "the 400 richest families have a combined wealth of $1.57 trillion more than the combined wealth of 50 percent of U.S. population"[44] and that "the top 1 percent took in 23.5 percent of [the] nation's pretax income in 2007—up from less than 9 percent in 1976."[45] In spite of the fact that every thirty-fourth wage earner in America in 2008 went during all of 2009 without earning a single dollar,[46] Wall Street handed out $150 billion to its executives.[47] As David DeGraw points out, "100 percent of these bonuses are a direct result of our tax dollars, so if we used this money to create jobs, instead of giving them to a handful of top executives, we could have paid an annual salary of $30,000 to 5 million people."[48] And as the "'bonus culture' of greed, ambition, and excess"[49] continues, middle- and working-class families are ending up in food pantries, homeless shelters, or worse.

Yet Lloyd Blankfein, the CEO of Goldman Sachs, claims that the "bonus culture" produced by the current crop of financial zombies is "doing God's work."[50] Without any irony intended, Blankfein publicly asserts this arrogant comment, knowing full well that under the grip of the recession caused by those "doing God's work," teachers are experiencing massive layoffs; public servants are taking salary and benefit cuts; schools are hemorrhaging under a lack of resources; and the war in Afghanistan endlessly siphons off financial resources needed by the federal and state governments to address the nation's housing, employment, and economic crises.

Under the reign of the punishing state, those experiencing poverty are seen as the problem and become an easy target for mobilizing middle-class fears about not just the poor, the disabled, immigrants, and others who might depend on social services, but also the social services themselves and the policies that make them possible. Even as inequality deepens and the ultrarich wreak havoc on the globe, the dominant media focus on so-called welfare cheaters, while right-wing politicians go out of their way to associate poverty and dependency with a culture of crime and immorality. The social state is portrayed as a "nanny state," and those who partake of its services are represented as childish, lazy, and lacking any sense of individual responsibility. One example of this discourse can be found in a statement by former Republican presidential candidate Mike Huckabee, who compared people with preexisting health conditions to burned-out houses. In this instance, Huckabee was criticizing Obama's health care plan, which requires insurance companies to cover people with preexisting conditions.[51]

We also see the attack on the poor and welfare policies being magnified as part of the right-wing call for austerity. Punitive sanctions against the poor combine with a kind of class and racial cleansing as right-wing politicians block legislation for schools to provide free meals to thousands of hungry children, eliminate public transportation systems, lay off thousands of civil servants, cancel school programs that benefit the poor, and ask parents to pay for school supplies.[52] As I argue throughout this book, the politics of austerity is not about rethinking priorities to benefit the public good. Instead, it has become part of a discourse of shame, one that has little to do with using indignation to imagine a better world. On the contrary, shame and humiliation are now used to wage a war on the poor rather than on poverty, on young people rather than on those economic and political forces that undermine their future, and on those considered other rather than on the underlying structures and ideologies of various forms of state and individual racism.

We need to return to Benjamin's angel of history in order to reimagine what it means to reconstruct a social state that invests in people rather than in the rich, megacorporations, the prison-industrial complex, and a permanent war economy. We need to imagine how the state can be refigured along with the very nature of politics and economics in order to eliminate structural inequality, racism, and militarism. Once again, Americans must recognize that something is "profoundly wrong with the way we live today"[53] and that the obsession with wealth, war, and violence is at odds with those democratic ideals often invoked in the name of freedom, justice, and equality.

Just as we need a new language for talking about public values, shared responsibilities, and the common good, we also need a language for connecting the war at home with the war abroad. War is rarely about real defense or national honor, as the wars in Iraq and Afghanistan demonstrate. Not only are these two wars draining the public treasury, they are also partly responsible for budget cuts at home that aim at balancing federal and state budgets on the backs of the poor, minority youth, working people, and the elderly. Robust war spending is matched by the massive cutting of school budgets at home. The United States spends $1.1 million per year to put a single soldier in Afghanistan, but refuses to bail out public schools, rescue universities that are suffering massive budget cuts, or reinvest in its crumbling national infrastructure. We offer paltry aid to support public libraries or to assist students who now absorb massive debts to finance their education, while potentially spending between $3.2 and $4 trillion to cover the wars in Iraq, Pakistan, Afghanistan, and other operations associated with the war on terror.[54] Instead of using these funds for crucial domestic programs that could develop jobs, public works programs, health initiatives, housing, and education, the punishing state, with its permanent war machine, spreads death and destruction through the organization and production of violence. The punishing state not only locks up more people than any other country in the world, but also, as Tom Englehardt states, "puts more money into the funding of war, our armed forces and the weaponry of war than the next 25 countries combined. We garrison the planet in a way no empire or nation in history has ever done."[55] With an imperialist mentality, war economy, and militaristic values ruling the United States, we see daily the destruction of human lives and the exacerbation of massive inequalities that now permeate every aspect of American life. War has become a poison that legitimates the corporate state, on the one hand, and works in tandem with the punishing state on the other. At the same time, it feeds an inequality that rots U.S. society from within as it turns over matters of democratic governance and rule to corporate swindlers, military leaders, and right-wing ideologues. Tony Judt gets it right when he argues that:

> Inequality, then, is not just unattractive in itself; it clearly corresponds to pathological social problems that we cannot hope to address unless we attend to their underlying cause. There is a reason why infant mortality, life expectancy, criminality, the prison population, mental illness, unemployment, obesity, malnutrition, teenage pregnancy, illegal drug use, economic insecurity, personal indebtedness and anxiety are so much more marked in the US and the UK than they are in continental Europe.... Inequality is corrosive. It rots societies from within. The impact of material differences takes a while to show up: but in due course competition for status and goods increases; people feel a growing sense of superiority (or inferiority) based on their possessions; prejudice towards those on the lower ranks of the social ladder hardens; crime spikes and the pathologies of social disadvantage become ever more marked. The legacy of unregulated wealth creation is bitter indeed.[56]

If we are to imagine another type of society than the one we have, we will have to once again put the social question on the political agenda in order to understand how "the pathologies of inequality and poverty—crime, alcoholism, violence and mental illness—have all multiplied commensurately,"[57] and how we might take up the challenge of addressing the symptoms of social dysfunction through a concerted effort to embrace communal freedom, social investments, social rights, civic duties, and a vocabulary for translating private troubles into public issues. The return of the social question necessitates invoking a public language and a new set of questions regarding "What should be done to alleviate the suffering and injustices to which the urban working masses [are] now exposed and how [is] the ruling elite of the day to be brought to see the need for change?"[58] The social question also demands that we make visible what C. Wright Mills calls the forces of "organized irresponsibility [that] prevail everywhere,"[59] which function to dissolve crucial social solidarities, undermine compassion, disparage mutual responsibility, and disband the bonds of social obligation itself.[60] But if we are to put the social question back on the agenda, we will first have to acknowledge, like Benjamin's angel of history, the "catastrophe that keeps piling wreckage upon wreckage."[61] And we must also acknowledge that catastrophe lies in a brutal and ruthless form of economic Darwinism that shreds the social fabric of the state, eviscerates the importance of the social question, and creates the conditions for a society resembling Thomas Hobbes's war of all against all, a survival-of-the-fittest social order in which the flight from freedom and responsibility becomes the default mechanism for upholding a machinery of exploitation, cruelty, inequality, and militarism.

Not only has the U.S. public lost its ability, perhaps even its will, to talk about public values such as sharing, caring, and preserving, but it can no longer distinguish between a market-driven society and a democratic society. As Sheldon Wolin has insisted, the supportive culture for a viable democracy—"a complex of beliefs, values and practices that nurture equality, cooperation and freedom"[62]—is incompatible with the market-driven values of neoliberalism and their emphasis on a crude consumerism, over-the-top materialism, brutal competition, a culture of lying, a possessive individualistic ethic, and an aggressive battle to privatize, deregulate, and commodify everything.

The promise of democracy and economic justice and social rights necessitates a new language of public purpose, a new rationality, and a formative culture embedded in democratic public values, collective struggles, and a social movement willing to fight for a new kind of politics, democracy, and future. We don't need privatized utopias, but models of a democratic society and social state in which public values and democratic interests are expressed in a range of economic, political, and cultural institutions. We need a new army of critical and passionate winged messengers, alert to the need for progressive social solidarities, social agency, collective action, and refusing to stare hopelessly at the rotting corpses, gated communities, and walking dead that turn the promise of democracy into an advertisement for global destruction.

Notes

1. I would like to thank Zygmunt Bauman for his thoughtful comments on this chapter. Of course, I am ultimately responsible for the narrative that unfolds.

2. Tony Judt, *Ill Fares the Land* (New York: Penguin, 2010), 119.

3. Walter Benjamin, "Theses on the Philosophy of History," *Illuminations: Essays and Reflections,* Hannah Arendt, ed. (New York: Schocken Books, 1968), 257–258.

4. See, for instance, the brilliant reading provided by O. K. Werckmeister, "Walter Benjamin's Angel of History, or the Transfiguration of the Revolutionary into the Historian," *Critical Inquiry* 22 (Winter 1996): 239–267.

5. Benjamin, "Theses on the Philosophy of History," 257.

6. This comes from a personal correspondence with Zygmunt Bauman dated January 2, 2011.

7. Ibid.

8. Terry Eagleton, "Reappraisals: What Is the Worth of Social Democracy?" *Harper's Magazine,* October 2010, 77. For an extended analysis of the importance of the social state, see Tony Judt, *Ill Fares the Land.* For a series of extended commentaries on the social state, see Zygmunt Bauman, "Freedom From, In and Through the State: T. H. Marshall's Trinity of Rights Revised," *Theoria* (December 2005): 13–27, online at http://www.berghahnbooksonline.com/journals/th/abs/2005/52-3/TH520303.html; Zygmunt Bauman, "Has the Future a Left?" *Soundings* 35 (Spring 2007), online at http://www.lwbooks.co.uk/journals/articles/bauman07.html; Zygmunt Bauman, *Liquid Times: Living in an Age of Uncertainty* (London: Polity Press, 2007); Zygmunt Bauman, *Consuming Life* (London: Polity Press, 2007); Zygmunt Bauman, "Happiness in a Society of Individuals," *Soundings* (Winter 2008): 19–28; and Zygmunt Bauman, *The Art of Life* (London: Polity Press, 2008).

9. Richard D. Wolff, "Austerity: Why and for Whom?" *In These Times,* July 15, 2010, online at http://www.inthesetimes.com/article/6232/austerity_why_and_for_whom/. For a full-length study of how neoliberalism caused the financial crisis, see Gerard Dumenil and Dominique Levy, *The Crisis of Neoliberalism* (Princeton, NJ: Princeton University Press, 2011).

10. Zygmunt Bauman, *The Art of Life,* 88.

11. Ibid.

12. Bauman, personal correspondence.

13. Zygmunt Bauman, *Consuming Life,* 140.

14. Achille Mbembe, "Necropolitics," trans. Libby Meintjes, *Public Culture* 15:1 (2003): 37.

15. Judt, *Ill Fares the Land.*

16. Zygmunt Bauman, *Living on Borrowed Time: Conversations with Citlali Rovirosa-Madrazo* (Cambridge: Polity Press, 2010), 4.

17. See Michael Edwards, "Pragmatic Witness: Debtor's Prison Making a Comeback?" September 30, 2010, online at http://whitewraithe.wordpress.com/2010/09/30/debtors-prison-making-a-comeback/.

18. Bauman, *Living on Borrowed Time,* 66.

19. David Harvey, "Organizing for the Anti-Capitalist Transition," *Monthly Review,* December 15, 2009, online at http://davidharvey.org/2009/12/organizing-for-the-anti-capitalist-transition.

20. Chris Serres and Glenn Howatt, "In Jail for Being in Debt," *Minnesota Star Tribune,* June 9, 2010, online at http://www.startribune.com/investigators/95692619.html.

21. Michelle Brown, *The Culture of Punishment: Prison, Society and Spectacle* (New York: New York University Press, 2009), 6–7.

22. Loic Wacquant, *Punishing the Poor: The Neoliberal Government of Social Insecurity* (Durham, NC: Duke University Press, 2009).

23. Eagleton, "Reappraisals," 77.

24. Adam Cohen, "Should Tennessee Fireman Have Let the House Burn?" *Time with CNN,* October 13, 2010, online at http://www.time.com/time/nation/article/0,8599,2025342,00.html.

25. Faiz Shakir et al., "Conservatism's Trial by Fire," *Progress Report,* October 7, 2010, online at http://groups.google.com/group/rec.gambling.poker/browse_thread/thread/d2f279e415868ffe.

26. Cohen, "Should Tennessee Fireman Have Let the House Burn?"

27. Tony Judt, "What Is Living and What Is Dead in Social Democracy?" *New York Review of Books,* vol. 56, no. 20, December 17, 2009, online at http://www.nybooks.com/articles/23519.

28. Zygmunt Bauman, *Liquid Fear* (Cambridge: Polity Press, 2006), 154–155.

29. Marc Lacey, "Arizona Cuts Financing for Transplant Patients," *New York Times,* December 2, 2010, A1.

30. Marc Lacey, "Transplants Cut, Arizona Is Challenged by Survivors," *New York Times,* December 18, 2010, A18.

31. Dpolitico, "Arizona Death Panels: State Revokes Funding for Heart Transplants, Opts to Save Squirrels," *End Politics As Usual,* November 17, 2010, online at http://www.endpoliticsasusual.com/2010/11/arizona-death-panels-state-revokes-funding-for-heart-transplants-opts-to-save-squirrels/.

32. Ibid.

33. Ibid.

34. Franklin D. Roosevelt, "State of the Union Message to

Congress—January 11, 1944," *The American Presidency Project.* Accessed December 30, 2010, from http://www.presidency.ucsb.edu/ws/index.php?pid=16518.

35. Bauman, *The Art of Life,* 41.

36. Slavoj Žižek, *First as Tragedy Then as Farce* (New York: Verso, 2009), 99–100.

37. Ibid.

38. Erik Eckholm, "Recession Raises Poverty Rate to a 15-Year High," *New York Times,* September 16, 2010, A1.

39. Les Christie, "Poverty in the U.S. Spikes," *CNN Money,* September 23, 2010, online at http://money.cnn.com/2010/09/16/news/economy/census_poverty_rate/index.htm.

40. David DeGraw, "The Economic Elite Have Engineered an Extraordinary Coup, Threatening the Very Existence of the Middle Class," *AlterNet,* February 15, 2010, online at http://www.alternet.org/story/145667/null.

41. Matt Taibbi, "The Tea Party Moron Complex," *Alter-Net,* November 14, 2010, online at http://www.alternet.org/teaparty/148855/taibbi:_the_tea_party_moron_complex.

42. David Cay Johnston, "Scary New Wage Data," *Tax Justice Network,* October 18, 2010, online at http://archive.truthout.org/robert-reich-the-perfect-storm64313.

43. Robert Reich, "The Perfect Storm," *TruthOut,* October 10, 2010, online at http://www.truth-out.org/robert-reich-the-perfect-storm64313.

44. David DeGraw, "The Richest 1% Have Captured America's Wealth—What's It Going to Take to Get It Back?" *AlterNet,* February 17, 2010, online at http://www.alternet.org/module/printversion/145705.

45. Frank Rich, "Who Will Stand Up to the Superrich?" *New York Times,* November 13, 2010, WK8.

46. Ibid.

47. DeGraw, "The Richest 1%."

48. Ibid.

49. Gesa Helms, Marina Vishmidt, and Lauren Berlant, "Affect and the Politics of Austerity: An Interview Exchange with Lauren Berlant," *Variant* 39/40 (Winter 2010): 3–6, online at http://www.variant.org.uk/39_40texts/Variant39_40.html#L1.

50. Douglas McIntyre, "Goldman Sachs CEO Blankfein Says Firm Is Doing 'God's Work,'" *Daily Finance,* November 9, 2009, online at http://www.dailyfinance.com/story/company-news/goldman-sachs-is-doing-gods-work/19228542/.

51. William Rivers Pitt, "Sick Bastards," *TruthOut,* September 22, 2010, online at http://www.truth-out.org/sick-bastards63456.

52. Michael Cooper, "Governments Go to Extremes as the

Downturn Wears On," *New York Times*, August 6, 2010, A1, A11; Paul Krugman, "America Goes Dark," *New York Times*, August 8, 2010, A19, online at http://www.nytimes.com/2010/08/09/opinion/09krugman.html.

53. Judt, *Ill Fares the Land*, 1–2.

54. See Neta C. Crawford and Catherine Lutz, "Economic and Budgetary Costs of the Wars in Afghanistan, Iraq, and Pakistan to the United States," *CostsOfWar.org* (Brown University's Watson Institute for International Studies), July 3, 2011, online at http://costsofwar.org/; Congressional Research Service Report for Congress, *The Cost of Iraq, Afghanistan, and Other Global War on Terror Operations Since 9/11* (Washington: Congressional Research Service, September 2010), online at http://www.fas.org/sgp/crs/natsec/RL33110.pdf.

55. Tom Engelhardt, "An American World War: What to Watch for in 2010," *TruthOut*, January 3, 2010, online at http://www.truth-out.org/topstories/10410vh4. For a detailed study of these issues, see Andrew J. Bacevich, *Washington Rules: America's Path to Permanent War* (New York: Metropolitan Books, 2010), and Chalmers Johnson, *Nemesis: The Last Days of the American Republic* (New York: Metropolitan Books, 2006).

56. For a recent detailed critique of inequality, see Richard Wilkinson and Kate Pickett, *The Spirit Level: Why More Equal Societies Almost Always Do Better* (London: Allen Lane, 2009). See also Dollars & Sense and United for a Fair Economy, eds., *The Wealth Inequality Reader*, 2nd edition (Boston: Dollars & Sense, 2008).

57. Judt, *Ill Fares the Land*, 175.

58. Ibid., 174.

59. C. Wright Mills, "The Powerless People: The Role of the Intellectual in Society," in C. Wright Mills, *The Politics of Truth: Selected Writings of C. Wright Mills* (New York: Oxford University Press, 2008), 18.

60. These ideas are taken from Stuart Hall in Len Terry, "Traveling 'The Hard Road to Renewal': A Continuing Conversation with Stuart Hall," *Arena Journal* 8 (1997): 39–58.

61. Benjamin, "Theses on the Philosophy of History," 257.

62. Sheldon S. Wolin, *Democracy Incorporated: Managed Democracy and the Specter of Inverted Totalitarianism* (Princeton, NJ: Princeton University Press, 2008), 260–261.

◇

2

The Crisis of Public Values in the Age of the New Media

The materialistic and selfish quality of contemporary life is not inherent in the human condition. Much of what appears "natural" today dates from the 1980s: the obsession with wealth creation, the cult of privatization and the private sector, the growing disparities of rich and poor. And above all, the rhetoric which accompanies these: uncritical admiration for unfettered markets, disdain for the public sector, the delusion of endless growth. We cannot go on living like this. The little crash of 2008 was a reminder that unregulated capitalism is its own worst enemy.

—*Tony Judt*[1]

The decay of democratic public values has become a serious crisis confronting U.S. politics. Although public values have for decades been in tension with dominant economic, political, and social forces, the notion of the common good seems no longer worthy of mobilizing a polity against the impassioned attacks of right-wing forces that have come to dominate political and cultural spheres in the United States. The neoliberal fervor for unbridled individualism—almost pathological in its disdain for community, public values, and the public good—has produced "a weakening of democratic pressures, a growing inability to act politically, [and] a massive exit from politics and from responsible citizenship."[2] When public values are invoked, to paraphrase Walter Benjamin, they appear less for their recognizability and relevance for the present than as a symbol of what has been irrevocably lost.[3] Public values along with the public good have been reduced to nostalgic reminders of another era—associated, for example, with the New Deal or the Great Society—in which the social contract was seen as crucial to meeting the needs of postwar Americans and fundamental to a substantive democratic order. Rather than viewed as a legacy that needs to be reclaimed, reimagined, and renewed, visions of the public good are consigned to the distant past, a passing curiosity like a museum piece perhaps worth viewing, but not worth struggling to revive as either an ideal or a reality. What is "new" about the long decline of public values in U.S. society is not that they are again under attack but that they have become weakened to the point of no longer inspiring outright popular uprisings in the face of more daring and destructive attacks by conservatives, right-wing politicians, and corporate power. When such values are attacked, the targets are groups who for decades have been largely immune to such attacks because they embody the most cherished ideals associated with democratic public service—public school teachers, public servants, and labor unions.

After decades of systematic dismantling, residual notions of anything public have become increasingly irrelevant to the existing contemporary neoliberal order, which slowly saps the foundation of social solidarity, unravels the bonds of social obligation, and insists on the ability of markets to solve all social and individual problems.[4] This might be why in the midst of an economic recession caused by the corrupt dealings of the banks, insurance companies, and hedge fund drones, the public believes that sacrifices have to be shared and that public employees have to give up some of their benefits, delay retirement, and accept lower wages. The general public almost never points the finger at powerful corporations or the elite rich, who seem immune from the shared-sacrifice argument and consequently are not asked to give up anything, including obscene tax breaks. In fact, they have accrued even more wealth and income while arrogantly ingratiating themselves in what is truly the second Gilded Age. Although income inequality has been on the rise in advanced industrial nations, it is most pronounced in the United States. In fact, as reported in the *Washington Post,* "In 2008, the last year for which data are available, for example, the top 0.1 percent of earners took in more than 10 percent of the personal income in the United States, including capital gains, and the top 1 percent took in more than 20 percent."[5] Moreover, executive pay is skyrocketing as is evidenced by the fact that "The annual 'Executive Excess' survey from the progressive Institute for Policy Studies last September found that back in the seventies, only a handful of top American executives earned more than thirty times what their workers made. In 2009, "CEOs of major US corporations averaged 263 times the average compensation of American workers." And a *USA Today* analysis earlier this year found that while median CEO pay jumped 27 percent last year, workers in private industry saw their salaries grow by just 2.1 percent.[6] Top salaries in the second Gilded Age not only promote massive amounts of inequality, they register how new concentrations of power produce levels of greed that appear to have no limits. How else to explain that "the pay of 2591 executives was up 13.9 percent in 2010. Total, before taxes: $14.3 billion, almost equal to the GDP of Tajikistan, population: more than seven million"?[7]

Under the regime of market fundamentalism, many institutions that were meant to limit human suffering and misfortune have been either weakened or abolished, as have many of those public spheres where private troubles could be understood as social problems and addressed as such.[8] Privatization has run rampant, engulfing institutions as different in their goals and functions as universities, on the one hand, and prisons, on the other. This shift was all part of a broader process of "reducing state support of social goods [and] means that states—the institutions best placed to defend the gains workers and other popular forces have made in previous struggles—are instead abandoning them."[9] As social problems were privatized and public spaces were commodified, there was an increased emphasis on devising individual solutions to socially produced problems, while at the same time market relations and the commanding institutions of capital were divorced from matters of politics, ethics, and responsibility. In these circumstances, notions of the public good, community, and the obligations of citizenship were replaced by the overburdened demands of individual responsibility and an utterly privatized ideal of freedom. A vision of the good society has been replaced with visions of individual happiness, characterized by an endless search for instant gratification.

One of the most devastating outcomes from this loss of public values is the diminished sense of obligation to care for anything other than our own personal interests. As Zygmunt Bauman points out, "just as we as individuals feel no responsibility toward the other, so does the sense of political responsibility for social problems weaken."[10] In the current market-driven society, with its ongoing uncertainties and collectively induced anxieties, disengagement from the demands of social responsibility and the bonds of solidarity has become commonplace. Core public values regarding compassion for the common good have been abandoned under the regime of a market society that promotes a survival-of-the-fittest economic doctrine. As Jeffrey Sachs points out, "Income inequality is at historic highs, but the rich claim they have no responsibility to the rest of society. They refuse to come to the aid of the destitute, and defend tax cuts at every opportunity. Almost everybody complains, almost everybody aggressively defends their own narrow, short-term interests, and almost everybody abandons any pretense of looking ahead or addressing the needs of others."[11] Consequently, our capacity to translate the personal suffering of others into a moral obligation for society as a whole has diminished, if not disappeared, under the conditions created by neoliberalism.

With the unfolding of the second Gilded Age in late 1970s, notions of the social state, with its language of the public good, social protections, shared responsibilities, public spheres, and economic rights appear to have been erased from the social landscape. Public commitment has been undermined in the face of a neoliberal regime in which politics both separates itself from corporate power and removes itself from the discourse of the common good, now defined mostly through the language of privatization, competitiveness, profitability, efficiency, and cost-benefit calculations. Conservatives and liberals alike seem to view public values, public spheres, and the notion of the common good as either a hindrance to the profit-seeking goals of a market-driven society or a drain on society, treated as a sign of weakness, if not pathology.[12]

As responsibility for the lives and humanity of others was removed from society's moral index and social protections—especially for those who are poor, unemployed, sick, homeless, single, or marginalized by race, gender, class, or citizenship—government and public services were dismissed as either producing outmoded bureaucracies or building dangerous and costly social formations. Public spheres that once offered at least the glimmer of progressive ideas, enlightened social policies, non-commodified values, and critical exchange have been increasingly commercialized or replaced by private spaces and settings whose ultimate fidelity is to expanding profit margins. For example, public schools are now removed from the language of equity and democracy; higher education is increasingly defined as another core element of corporate power and culture; and public spaces such as libraries are detached from the language of public discourse, viewed increasingly as a waste of taxpayer money. No longer vibrant political spheres and ethical sites, public spaces are reduced to dead spaces in which it becomes almost impossible to construct those modes of knowledge, communication, agency, and meaningful interventions necessary for an aspiring democracy.

Instead of public spheres that promote dialogue, debate, and arguments with supporting evidence, we have entertainment spheres that infantilize almost everything they touch, while offering opinions that utterly disregard reason, truth, and civility. One example is the rise of those anti-public spheres now controlled by right-wing corporate power and religious fanatics, including talk radio, Fox News, and Pat Robertson's Christian Broadcasting Network.[13] Political discourse has come under the sway of multiple forms of fundamentalism, becoming oriented toward militarized, privatized, and racialized values, divorced from any notion of democratic governance or public welfare. Violence saturates the culture; a brutalizing masculinity and racist discourse fueled by religious zealotry and fear cancels out a respect for the disadvantaged other; and a collective ignorance is nurtured with the claim that intelligence and thoughtfulness should be dismissed as a form of elitism, or worse, subject to the logic of commodification.

The goal of making the world a better place has been replaced by dystopian narratives about how to survive alone in a world whose destruction is just a matter of time. The lure of a better and more just future has given way under the influence of neoliberalism to questions of mere survival. Entire populations, once protected by the social contract, are now considered disposable, relegated to the garbage dump of a society that equates one's humanity exclusively with the ability to consume.[14] Immigrants are now viewed as a social virus and increasingly subject to violations of their civil liberties and police brutality.[15] Impoverished sections of urban centers throughout the United States take on the appearance of cities devastated by war and other major disasters. Poor black and brown youth are relegated to fodder for the military interventions in Iraq and Afghanistan or make up a disproportionate number of those who are either incarcerated or under the control of the criminal justice system.[16] Death, fear, and insecurity trump important questions about what it means to apprehend the conditions to live a good life in common with others. Not only is the issue of the good life and the conditions that make it possible often lost in the babble of the infotainment state and the new media, but the market values that produced the 2008 economic crisis have so devalued the concept and practice of democracy that Americans find it hard even to define its meaning outside of the sham of money-driven elections, the obligations of consumerism, and the freedom to shop.

Inequality and commodification mutually reinforce each other under the regime of neoliberalism, as the gap between the rich and the poor widens dramatically and commercial carpet bombing by an unscrupulous advertising industry reaches into every aspect of daily life.[17] At the same time, as so many material aspects of everyday life are irrevocably transformed by a growing inequality, the broader culture shifts attention away from political engagement and social relations toward the alleged panacea of individual consumption.[18] But the reality produced by the stark demands of efficiency, downsizing, and deregulation leaves more than 14 million unemployed, several million more underemployed, and more than 45 million Americans living in poverty and destitution.[19] As the public pedagogy of market fundamentalism wages a war against all social solidarities, each individual feels isolated and trapped within his or her own fears, insecurities, and anxieties, while a smokescreen billows up to conceal the systemic problems caused by "corporate domination, abuse and greed."[20] Public reeducation by market-driven forces depoliticizes the language and culture that shape people's realities and identities, divorces private concerns from public concerns, and increasingly replaces the once prevalent concept of *citizen* with that of *consumer.* Under such circumstances, the practice of consumer wastefulness is paralleled by what Bauman calls the "the 'human waste' disposal industry,"[21] in which millions of people, often already marginalized because of their class and race, are viewed as redundant or a burden on the economy and labeled "disposable." In addition to contributing to the production of disposable populations, now cut adrift from any anchor that could provide social security, neoliberalism "eliminates the existential security that rests on collective foundations"[22] and, in doing so, encourages a form of hyperindividualism, economic Darwinism, and culture of cruelty in which everyone is self-absorbed and neglectful of the needs of others. Under the current regime of neoliberalism, the crisis of inequality is inextricably connected to the crisis of public values, which contributes to the broader crisis of the social and how we think about the meaning of politics itself.[23]

Subordinating the Social

In the last decade, the representative functions of democracy have been severely compromised in light of a political system whose policies are shaped by powerful corporations and the imperatives of the rich. Also contributing to the decline and dysfunction of representative democracy are a sham electoral system and cultural apparatus intimately tied to wealth and power. Eric Alterman argues in *The Nation* that the system is rigged—controlled by the rich in order to benefit the wealthy and the powerful—and because the system is viewed as unalterable, its eventual demise is deemed less a matter of politics than of fate, normalized in the media and denied the possibility of struggle and change. Alterman further insists that "Many of the myriad points of democratic dysfunction of the American political system . . . are the result of the peculiar commercial and ideological structure of our media, which not only frame our political debate but also determine which issues will be addressed."[24] In this instance, the dominant media largely function as a moral anesthesia and political firewall that legitimate a ruthless and fraudulent free-market system, while failing to make visible the workings of a casino capitalism that rejects as weakness any measure of compassion, care, trust, and vulnerability. As the anti-public values and interests of the market become a template for all of society, the only institutions, social relations, public spheres, and modes of agency that matter are those that pay homage to the rule of mobile capital and the interests of financial titans. What the ongoing financial crisis reveals has less to do with the so-called greed of Wall Street moguls than with the increasing fragility of a market-driven system that produces inequalities in every sphere of life, making its paean to democracy and the good life a pure sham.

Although the decline and devaluation of democratic public values in U.S. society—readily evident in the dominant media culture—has many causes, one important factor rarely addressed is what John Clarke has called "the anti-social character of neoliberalism."[25] The ongoing attack on the social in the United States has taken on the status of a low-intensity war, starting with the election of Ronald Reagan in 1980, though its emergent tendencies were part of U.S. politics long before the emergence of the second Gilded Age. Reagan's infamous claim that "government is not the solution to our problems; government is the problem" represented an attack on public values and social rights as well as a full-fledged attempt to undermine all of those social relations, spaces, and spheres organized to define the public good outside of the primacy of privatization and commodification.[26] The attack on all forms of social protections and rights was further intensified with the unchallenged reign of neoliberal policies that were fully endorsed and supported both during and after Reagan's time in the White House.[27]

According to Clarke, the subordination of the social by neoliberalism takes place in a variety of ways: elimination of social protections for labor; privatization of the social by turning public goods into for-profit opportunities; subjugation of social needs and policies to the imperatives of economic competitiveness and capital accumulation; erosion of collective provisions that provide "for welfare, well-being, security, and care," while placing the burden for such provisions on individuals and families; the narrowing of the social by downsizing it into "meaner, degraded or recitalist forms";

and, finally, the economizing of the social, which refers to "the construction of new subjectivities, [that is] producing individuals who think of themselves in economic terms—as entrepreneurial, calculating selves whose world is structured through contractual or quasi-contractual relationships."[28] Also ensuing from neoliberalism's domination of the social, as Loic Wacquant points out, is the merger of social welfare and crime control—we are witnessing the expansion of a penal pedagogy, models of law and order, and the punishing state in order to address social problems, regulate the conduct of the poor, and manage those populations considered disposable.[29]

The various facets of subordinating the social extend from matters of legitimating new forms of power to reinventing the social and constructing the formative culture necessary to produce the kinds of agents and subjects who define themselves within, rather than against, the neoliberal view of the world.[30] Recognizing how the social is being subordinated to market-driven interests points to the need to create new spaces and the vocabulary for a politics in which a plurality of public spheres can promote, express, and create the public values necessary to a thriving democracy. Reclaiming the social as part of a democratic imaginary entails making the learning process central not simply to social change but to the struggle to democratize the very character of U.S. politics, institutional power, and public discourse.

Eroding Public Spheres and the Logic of Depoliticization

As the dominant culture is emptied of any substantive meaning and filled with the spectacles of the entertainment industry, the banality of celebrity culture, and a winner-take-all consumer mentality, the American people lose both the languages and the public spheres in which they can actually think politics, "respond energetically and imaginatively to new challenges,"[31] and collectively organize in order to influence the commanding ideologies, social practices, and institutions that bear down daily on their lives. Missing from neoliberal society are those spheres or liminal spaces where people can develop what C. Wright Mills called "the sociological imagination." According to Mills,

The sociological imagination enables its possessor to understand the larger historical scene in terms of its meaning for the inner life and the external career of a variety of individuals. It enables him to take into account how individuals, the welter of their daily experience, often become falsely conscious of their position. Within that welter, the framework of modern society is sought, and within the framework the psychologies of a variety of men and women are formulated. By such means the personal uneasiness of individuals is focused upon explicit troubles and the indifference of publics is transformed into involvement with public issues. The first fruit of this imagination—and the first lesson of the social science that embodies it—is the idea that the individual can understand his own experience and gauge his own fate only by locating himself within his period, that he can know his own chances in life only by becoming aware of those of all individuals in his circumstances.[32]

One consequence of the loss of those public spheres that nurture the sociological imagination and the possibility of democratic politics is the ongoing depoliticization of the U.S. public and the normalization of a market-driven society. Numbed into a moral and political coma, large segments of the U.S. public and media have not only renounced the political obligation to question authority but also the moral obligation to care for the fate and well-being of others.[33] Thoughtfulness is often ridiculed, while responsibility turns inward, mimicking the arrogance and narcissism that marked the second Gilded Age that began in the 1970s and has once again returned with a vengeance. The flight from responsibility and critical thought is further accentuated by the toxic fog of *ethical tranquilization*[34] that overtakes the society. This is not surprising in a culture that for the most part uncritically accepted the heralding of postindustrial capitalism as the end of ideology and history and, in doing so, effectively made power invisible by removing the structures and institutions of neoliberal society from a comprehension of the historical struggles out of which they developed.[35] In such instances, depoliticization works its way through the social order, removing social relations from the configurations of power that shape them and substituting "emotional and personal vocabularies for political ones in formulating solutions to political problems."[36]

The process of depoliticization is amplified through the on-going privatization and commercialization of formerly public spaces, which provide no support for citizen-based struggles and the expressive capacities required for public exchange. Under such circumstances, there is a "dissipation of the courage to ... rally in the name of a society more hospitable to human needs ... a weakening of democratic pressures, a growing inability to act politically [and] a massive exit from politics and from responsible citizenship."[37] In a culture where the gap between nation-based politics and power in the form of financial capital flows beyond the reach of state governance, political agency, as the capacity to both analyze and question existing social forces and then transform them, has become troubling and problematic. Central to matters of reclaiming agency and those public spheres that help sustain a larger democratic order is rethinking the potential role of the new media as offering the rudiments of a forma-tive culture that fosters justice, compassion, and a concern for others. But before examining the democratic potential and educational value of the new media, I will first address the notion of a formative culture and how public pedagogy operates within such a culture to either generate or destroy a viable understanding of democratic politics.

The Crisis of a Democratic Formative Culture

What is particularly troubling in U.S. society is the absence of a formative culture necessary to construct questioning agents who are capable of dissent and collective action in an increasingly imperiled democracy. Sheldon Wolin rightly insists that the creation of a democratic formative culture is fundamental to enabling political agency and a critical un-derstanding of what it means to sustain a viable democracy. According to Wolin,

> democracy is about the conditions that make it possible for ordinary people to better their lives by becoming political beings and by making power responsive to their hopes and needs. What is at stake in democratic politics is whether ordinary men and women can recognize that their concerns

are best protected and cultivated under a regime whose actions are governed by principles of commonality, equality, and fairness, a regime in which taking part in politics becomes a way of staking out and sharing in a common life and its forms of self-fulfillment. Democracy is not about bowling together but about managing together those powers that immediately and significantly affect the lives and circumstances of others and one's self.[38]

Wolin does not limit democracy merely to participation and accountability, nor does he connect it exclusively to matters of wealth redistribution and economic justice, though the importance of these issues should not be underestimated. Matters of justice, equality, and political participation are foundational in a democracy, but it is important to recognize that they have to be supplemented by a vibrant formative culture for a democracy to flourish. The institutions and practices of a formative culture that provide modes of thought and agency that constitute and support the very foundations of the culture are also crucial to imagining and sustaining the dreamscape of an aspiring democracy. Wolin makes this clear in his insistence that "If democracy is about participating in self-government, its first requirement is a supportive culture, a complex of beliefs, values, and practices that nurture equality, cooperation, and freedom. A rarely discussed but crucial need of a self-governing society is that the members and those they elect to office tell the truth."[39]

The importance of formative culture as a mode of civic education in the shaping of democratic values and critical agents can be found in the work of many theorists, extending from C. Wright Mills and Raymond Williams to Cornelius Castoriadis and Sheldon Wolin. What all of these theorists share is the recognition that pedagogy is central to any viable notion of politics, and that various cultural and media sites help produce new subjects who are summoned to inhabit the values, dreams, and social relations of an already established social order. All of these theorists understand that the educational force of the wider culture and the sites in which it is produced and distributed demand a radical rethinking of politics itself. They all argue that education in the broadest sense must be viewed as essential to making connections between learning and social change, especially in light of the centrality of the new media—and the role of the Internet in particular—in comprehending the politics of the present historical conjuncture and the need to assert the claims of justice and democracy.

Each of these theorists recognizes the political importance of understanding how different sites of public pedagogy transmit different types of knowledge, which necessitates a critical analysis of how people learn through cultural mechanisms outside of traditional sites of schooling.[40] For instance, Raymond Williams coined the important term *permanent education* in order to analyze the various ways in which learning takes place in diverse sites, employs complex technologies, and produces varied circuits of power that constitute this form of public pedagogy outside of the institutions of formal schooling. According to Williams, the notion of permanent education not only points to the multiplicity of settings in which pedagogical engagement is initiated, but also lies at the heart of any viable notion of cultural politics. Williams argues that "What [permanent education] valuably stresses is the educational force of our whole social and cultural experience. It is therefore concerned, not only with continuing education, of a formal or informal kind, but with what the whole environment, its institutions and relationships, actively and profoundly teaches."[41] In this instance, education is viewed as a cultural pedagogical practice that takes place across multiple sites. Williams signals how, within diverse contexts, the public pedagogy of the wider culture makes us both subjects of and subject to relations of power.

C. Wright Mills, developing Antonio Gramsci's understanding of the importance of education as a crucial element of politics, power, and domination, was also concerned with how what he calls "the cultural apparatus" produces new modes of language, consciousness, agency, and social relations. According to Mills,

> This apparatus is composed of all the organizations and milieux in which artistic, intellectual, and scientific work goes on, and by which entertainment and information are produced and distributed. It contains an elaborate set of institutions: of schools and theaters, newspapers and census bureaux, studios, laboratories, museums, little magazines, radio networks. It contains truly fabulous agencies of exact information and of

trivial distraction, exciting objects, lazy escape, and strident advice. Inside this apparatus, standing between men and events, the images, meanings, slogans that define the world in which men live are organized and compared, maintained and revised, lost and cherished, hidden, debunked, celebrated. It is the source of the Human Variety—of styles of living and of ways to die.[42]

Mills did not believe that human beings acted only from pressures stemming from the economy and the forces of production. On the contrary, he was convinced that the cultural apparatus that mediates between consciousness and everyday life is central to performing the ideological labor of producing politicized subjects and supporting those public spheres where cultural forms, norms, and social relations make possible a culture of critique, interrogation, and collective resistance. For Mills, people live in worlds of meaning and social relations largely framed by a culture that traffics between meaning and authority, while also guiding experience and expropriating "the very chance to have experiences that can rightly be called our own."[43] The political importance of the cultural apparatus is obvious in the following statement. Mills writes,

> our standards of credibility, our definitions of reality, our modes of sensibility—as well as our immediate opinions and images—are determined much less by any pristine experience than by our exposure to the output of the cultural apparatus. This apparatus is the seat of civilization, which, in Matthew Arnold's phrase, is "the humanization of man in society." It is in terms of some such conception as this apparatus that the politics of culture may be understood.[44]

The great philosopher of democracy Cornelius Castoriadis added to this perspective the idea that for democracy to work not only do people have to have a passion for public values, social responsibility, and participation in society, but they also need to have access to those public spaces that guarantee the rights of free speech, dissent, and critical dialogue. Castoriadis recognized that at the heart of such public spaces is a formative culture that creates citizens who are critical thinkers capable of "putting existing institutions into

question so that democracy again becomes society's movement of self institution—that is to say, a new type of regime
in the full sense of the term."[45] For Castoriadis, people need
to be educated both as a condition of autonomy and for the
sustainability of democratization as an ongoing movement.
Not only does a substantive democracy demand citizens
capable of self-criticism and social criticism, but it also requires a formative culture in which people are provided with
the knowledge and skills to be able to participate in such a
society. According to Castoriadis,

> we cannot ignore—it's the least that can be said—that these
> equal individuals, whom we want to participate equally in
> power, are in each case codetermined in a decisive manner
> by society and by its institution, by … their education in the
> largest sense of the word. What are the implications of an
> education which aims at rendering all individuals fit, to the
> greatest extent possible, to participate in a common govern-
> ment? We must come back once again to Aristotle, who was
> acquainted quite well with this form of education, calling it
> the paideia pros ta koina—civic education—and considering
> it the essential dimension of justice.[46]

Castoriadis argued that with the rise of a dominant cultural
apparatus and the growing failure of schooling to provide a
civic education, people too often inhabit "a state of political
impassivity, privatization, irresponsibility, cynicism, and
indifference toward matters of public and political interest
… they possess an attitude toward their private and public
life which is more or less a state of indolence into television
and consumer masturbation."[47] Castoriadis believed that the
crisis of public values, public space, and democracy demands
a reclaiming of the importance of education as a foundation
for rethinking the very meaning of politics. He insisted that
although public spheres are crucial to a democracy, they
"are not just a matter of legal provisions guaranteeing rights
of free speech," but part of a broader struggle for the conditions that enable critical thought, judgment, choice, and
self-reflection, all of which provide the conditions for critical
agency and for public spheres to exist.[48] Ultimately, Castoriadis insisted that any discussion about democracy has to
be grounded in a broader understanding of civic education

as the foundation for enabling people to govern rather than simply be governed.

The writings of Williams, Mills, Castoriadis, and Wolin outline the importance of addressing issues of language, meaning, and culture as crucial to the task of rethinking the relationships among politics, agency, and power. Culture and its diverse storehouse of imagery, sound, and signification constitute the conditions for modes of autonomy and critical agency. Politics becomes dysfunctional without a supportive culture to provide the conditions for people to become self-critical, reflexive, and socially responsible. How individuals think about public values is not a question that focuses merely on the effects of the new and old media. On the contrary, it is fundamentally a political issue that can only be understood by analyzing the totality of a society and how it defines itself and the social relations that give it meaning.

What is often missing from any critique of neoliberalism is an account of the role and power represented by a formative culture and public pedagogy, both of which currently provide legitimacy for the subjects, values, and social relations crucial to market fundamentalism and market democracy. The formative culture and public pedagogy produced by the cultural apparatuses of neoliberal society do more than erase any vestige of self-regulation and public accountability. More insidiously, they also eliminate the language of self-reflection along with any form of productive discourse about the common good, public welfare, and providing for all the equality, justice, and dignity that make life worth living. Market-driven culture rejects the assumption that freedom is a shared experience in which self-interest is subordinated to the affirmation of public values. Reclaiming these values must begin with a concept of social responsibility that prioritizes the recognition and transformation of the conditions that make the survival of others precarious. As Judith Butler eloquently states,

> Precariousness implies living socially, that is, the fact that one's life is always in some sense in the hands of the other. It implies exposure both to those we know and to those we do not know; a dependency on people we know, or barely know, or know not at all. Reciprocally, it implies being impinged upon by the exposure and dependency of others, most of whom

remain anonymous. These are not necessarily relations of love or even of care, but constitute obligations toward others, most of whom we cannot name and do not know, and who may or may not bear traits of familiarity to an established sense of who "we" are. In the interest of speaking in common parlance, we could say that "we" have such obligations to "others" and presume that we know who "we" are in such an instance. The social implication of this view, however, is precisely that the "we" does not, and cannot, recognize itself, that it is riven from the start, interrupted by alterity, as Levinas has said, and the obligations "we" have are precisely those that disrupt any established notion of the "we."[49]

Democracy thrives on dissent. But dissent and critical citizenship cannot take place in a society marked by a widening gap between political democracy and socioeconomic capacities. Inequality is not just an inevitable outgrowth of a market-driven economy. It is an economic and political toxin that disdains public values, destroys human lives, divides populations, and corrodes societies from within. As Tony Judt points out,

> Economic disadvantage for the overwhelming majority translate[s] into ill health, missed educational opportunity and—increasingly—the familiar symptoms of depression: alcoholism, obesity, gambling and minor criminality.... Inequality, then, is not just unattractive in itself; it clearly corresponds to pathological social problems that we cannot hope to address unless we attend to their underlying cause. There is a reason why infant mortality, life expectancy, criminality, the prison population, mental illness, unemployment, obesity, malnutrition, teenage pregnancy, illegal drug use, economic insecurity, personal indebtedness and anxiety are so much more marked in the US and the UK than they are in continental Europe.[50]

The neoliberal adulation of wealth for its own sake, along with the growing dominance of violence, selfishness, materialism, and a culture of cruelty, is producing a lost generation of young people, a multitude of disposable individuals and groups, and a culture of deepening collective cynicism. It is also undermining whatever language is necessary to recognize the importance of public spheres that can counter the antidemocratic values, social relations, and representations that now dominate the landscape of U.S. political, cultural, and economic institutions. Any discussion about the decline of public values and the new media in the United States has to engage the performative power of neoliberalism as a mode of public pedagogy in the current historical conjuncture. At the same time, the issue of how the new social media can or might be understood for its potential as a counter-public sphere must become central to how politics is rethought in terms of its democratic possibilities for the twenty-first century.

The New Media and Public Values

The call for a revitalized politics grounded in an effective democracy is one point of entry in challenging the culture of neoliberalism. Instead of the fulfillment of the utopian promises made by neoliberal capital, people around the world increasingly face an all-consuming emphasis on insecurity, market relations, commercialization, privatization, and the creation of a global economy of part-time and itinerant workers. Initiating the challenge to neoliberalism's dystopian reality is important because it confronts Americans with the problem of developing those public spheres—such as the old and new media, higher education, and other cultural institutions—that provide the conditions for creating citizens who are capable of exercising their freedoms, competent to question the basic assumptions that govern political life, and skilled enough to participate in developing social movements that will enable them to shape the basic social, political, and economic orders that govern their lives.

In spite of the fact that some notions of the public good have been recalled from exile in light of the economic recession and the collective resistance being mobilized among workers, students, and others in defense of social protections and the most basic elements of the common good, many young people and adults today still view the private as the only space in which to imagine any sense of hope, pleasure, or possibility. Paradoxically, the expansion of the ideology of privatization through the public sector is made all the more powerful by the erosion of those intimate spaces that once offered some refuge from the market-driven values of the larger society. How else to understand a culture in which thoughtfulness is sacrificed to speed and multitasking and identities are defined through logos, brands, and labels? The domain of the private is increasingly erased through the ubiquitous presence of television in the home as well as the new electronic communication systems made possible by portable computers, wireless Internet connectivity, instant video and text messaging, surveillance technologies, and various mobile applications that unite humans and machines so as to infiltrate even the spaces and moments of personal reflection necessary to nurture critical modes of individual and social agency. The speed, rhythms, and modes of appropriation of the new electronic media, as Jacques Derrida has shown, work to undermine institutions and make critical thought and democratic speech difficult because of their relentless ability to colonize and commodify all aspects of everyday life.[51]

We live in a media-saturated culture in which the proliferation of the new, the emphasis on flexibility, and the rapid pace of change prevent experiences from crystalizing, events from being seriously discussed, and commitments to a just society from developing. Market forces continue to focus on the related issues of consumption, excessive profits, and fear. Reduced to the act of consuming, citizenship is "mostly about forgetting, not learning,"[52] despite the hyped-up and increasing appeal to bear collectively the burden of hard times—a burden that always seems to fall on the shoulders of working people but not on the banks or other commanding financial institutions that owe their survival to government bailouts. At the same time, governments and corporations incessantly work together to limit Internet freedom through censorship and surveillance while allowing advertising to permeate every corner of cyberspace.

As both physical and virtual spaces are increasingly undermined as sites for activating our political sensibilities and conceptualizing ourselves as critical citizens, the emancipatory possibilities of the new and old media get lost or buried in a society in which the lack of justice rises proportionately to the lack of political imagination and collective hope.[53] We live at a time when the forces and advocates of a market-driven fundamentalism and militarism not only resist all attempts to revive the culture of politics as an ethical response to the demise of democratic public life but also aggressively wage a war against the very possibility of creating non-commodified public spheres and forums that could provide the conditions for critical education, while also linking learning to social change, political agency to the defense of public goods, and intellectual courage to the refusal to surrender knowledge to the highest bidder. At the same time as we must acknowledge the challenges facing a technologically mediated democratic transformation, any progressive understanding of politics must reject the cynical assumption that the possibility for a democratically inspired new media is in terminal arrest. The new media occupy a space in the everyday life of Western societies that cannot be ignored—whether it "may lead to a public sphere of democratic discourse remains to be seen."[54] What has been made perfectly clear as a result of the new information communication revolution is the need for a broader understanding of how to think about politics and how to imagine a new conception for the public sphere.

How we might rethink the nature of politics and public values in light of the emergence of the new media poses a number of questions and challenges. I believe that it is pointless to define the media solely in terms of its technological advances, whether referring to the compression of time and space, the possibilities envisioned for new modes of communication, or the ability to access an abundance of information almost instantly. What seems more crucial than any of these concerns is to try to understand the new media within larger social, political, and economic forces that produce particular forms of agency that can mediate, support, or obliterate questions about the relevance of public values and social responsibility. The central question should be *how do we imagine the new media and their underlying communication systems as contributing to a distinctly different public sphere that offers the promise of recasting modes of agency and politics outside of the neoliberal ideology and disciplinary apparatus that now dominate contemporary culture?* Of course, we have had a glimpse of how the new media can be used for progressive purposes to mobilize populist grassroots movements, given the ways in which Barack Obama used it to rally young people, liberals, and independent voters in the 2008 presidential election.

Under the regime of neoliberalism, U.S. society has been transformed from a society of producers into a society of consumers.[55] Consequently, the social spaces that individuals now inhabit are dominated by commodities, and the unattached and uncommitted individual is now largely recast as the new symbol of consumer sovereignty and preferred model of agency.[56] Consumer culture has become a powerful framing mechanism for shaping the contours of the new media and information communication systems. In many cases everything from the Internet to social networking sites operates in a moral void, mimicking the ongoing infatuation with "wealth, sexual conquest, and fame" that dominate celebrity culture.[57] Facebook, Twitter, MySpace, and other social networks are largely shaped by endless bouts of naval gazing, bullying, and a relentless stream of self-promoting narratives that range from the trivial and boring to the obscene.[58] Increasingly such sites are being critiqued as a form of addiction for many young people.[59] Chris Hedges goes so far as to claim that not only has the Internet been hijacked by corporate interests, but it is also "forming anonymous crowds that vent collective rage, intolerance, and bigotry. These virtual slums do not expand communication or dialogue. They do not enrich our culture. They create a herd mentality in which those who express empathy for 'the enemy'—and the liberal class is as guilty of this as the right wing—are denounced by their fellow travelers for their impurity."[60]

This argument is repeated in a widely circulated article by Malcolm Gladwell, published by the influential magazine, *The New Yorker.*[61] Gladwell claims that the digital democracy promised by the new tools of the social media is not only misleading but counterproductive to a democracy and informed social action. According to Gladwell, the new media actually undermine social activism by promoting weak, if not trivial, ties between people, while largely ignoring important social problems. According to Gladwell, Twitter, Facebook, Second Life, and other social networks have little to do with the strong commitments, modes of deeply felt solidarity, and centrally organized hierarchies that characterized social movements such as the Civil Rights Movements of the 1960s. In the end, Gladwell concludes that social networking does more to increase the technological efficiency, rationality, and antidemocratic elements of the existing social order than empower dissidents or social movements. Although Gladwell is right to be suspicious of any wild utopian claims for the Internet and new media, he fails to address the pedagogical role the new media can play in producing a formative culture that disrupts corporate and government controlled media and makes social action possible. Gladwell dismisses the new media because he argues they do not produce the social action he celebrates in the 1960s Civil Rights Movement, but his view overlooks the educational value of such media in understanding and challenging the modes of knowledge and symbolic expression through which power often circulates in contemporary society. Nowhere is this oversight more obvious than in the recent protests in London and the uprisings in Egypt, Tunisia, Libya, Syria, and a number of other Middle Eastern countries. All of these protests were organized by young people who used the Internet along with Facebook, Twitter, and other social networks both to defy government power and, in the case of Tunisia and Egypt, to overthrow corrupt authoritarian governments. Gladwell seriously underestimates the importance of the new media in creating the formative culture and public values that might enable such action to happen. Although such media offer no political guarantees, they must be understood in terms of the power relations that employ them. By failing to grasp how the new media combine the political and the pedagogical, Gladwell fails to grasp how the existing use of the new media might not only produce modes of resistance, but assist governments, corporations, and other dominant institutions to produce and sustain conservative formative cultures and public pedagogies that are already in place. Gladwell de-romanticizes the often extravagant claims made for the new media, but in doing so, he ultimately cancels out his own critique by completely depoliticizing it as both a site for the practice of freedom and a critical form of public pedagogy.

Needless to say, the Internet offers a plethora of opportunities that includes everything from providing online educational opportunities for individuals living in remote areas to revolutionizing how doctors interact with each other and their patients. One example of how the new media can provide a formative culture that makes social action possible can be seen in the release by *WikiLeaks* of more than 91,000 classified military records on the war in Afghanistan. Such records are important because they largely serve to challenge many of the official government narratives used to legitimize and continue the war. The leaking of the Afghan war diaries speaks to the power of the Internet to make large amounts of information immediately available on the Web. More crucially, it also raises important questions about the new media and the role they might play in keeping citizens informed about decisions, policies, and events that bear down in powerful ways on their lives and the lives of others. In addition, there are many productive practices taking place on social networking sites that range from bringing extended families together to groups using such sites for political organization to individuals posting critical views on a variety of subjects. Yet, the emancipatory dimensions of the Internet and the information communication revolution seem to diminish next to the burgeoning presence of those forces aligned with state oppression, marketing tactics, and corporate-driven policies and practices. Moreover, the high-tech environment of the network society is largely controlled by transnational corporations and national governments that display an utter disregard for public values such as compassion, trust, sharing, honesty, and community building.[62]

For those who praise the technological wonders of the new information and communication age, there is often a ghostly presence, often left unmentioned, of antidemocratic corporate power in the United States that commodifies everything, including the ubiquitous technologies driving cyberspace.[63] Craig Calhoun reminds us that the new information technologies "are powerful, but not all powerful [and that they] are introduced into a world of existing social relations, culture, capitalism, and inequalities. These [for the most part] shape what will be made of it."[64] Whether the information highway, technoculture, and the digital revolution will provide gateways to new and more democratic public spheres remains to be seen. The Internet not only provides support for a vast array of global and local resistance movements, it also deploys "as much and as often a good deal more resources ... in support of global capitalism."[65] Despite or perhaps because of these inherent contradictions of the new media, the ghostly presence of a neoliberal politics haunting the utopian hopes of a new information world order demands that we take seriously the obligation to think from "another space for democracy."[66] Moreover, along with the much-touted growing technological achievements in the realm of cyberspace, there is a larger social order characterized by the emergence of the prison as a core political institution in U.S. society; the growing and obscene gap between the rich and the poor; and the ever-expanding culture of fast time, delete buttons, unrestrained pleasure, short-term advantage, and the celebrated avoidance of any relationship that demands a commitment or sense of social responsibility.[67] Given how neoliberal politics provides the framing mechanisms that shape the digital world of PDAs, smart phones, and computers, it becomes difficult, though far from impossible, to imagine how the new media can become a tool for democratic empowerment.

The new information technologies can only be judged within the power relations and dominant ideologies and values that frame how they are defined and used within the larger society. As a source of great hopes and equally distressing disappointments, the new media offer no political or social guarantees, although the proliferating modes of information and communication appear to represent a social existence that is here to stay. Many educators, social activists, and individuals are actively rewriting the rules for creating and using the new media. Any movement that connects the new techno culture with democratic values must begin by reclaiming the concept of the public sphere as a space in which the education and the communicative work of democracy take place.[68] Challenging the framing mechanisms and institutional structures of neoliberalism has to be high on the list of any attempt to shake the Internet and new media free from the overpowering influence of oppressive corporate and state power. At the same time, state authoritarianism has to be collectively resisted in its attempts to shut down the use of the Internet and the new media, especially when they are used to open up new spaces for critical dialogue and dissent. This suggests a political and a pedagogical struggle, not merely over the use of the technology, but over the public values and modes of identity that construct and mediate new forms of agency and social interaction.

Moreover, it is a mistake to believe that community building can be an exclusively virtual affair or that the current claims for online community building should go uncontested. Sherry Turkle observes a tendency among students who spend most of their time living in the virtual world of the Internet: They not only deny the pleasures of the body and intimacy but also forego the obligations of friendship. Turkle explains,

> What I'm seeing is a generation that says consistently, "I would rather text than make a telephone call." Why? It's less risky. I can just get the information out there. I don't have to get all involved; it's more efficient. I would rather text than see somebody face to face. There's this sense that you can have the illusion of companionship without the demands of friendship. The real demands of friendship, of intimacy, are complicated. They're hard. They involve a lot of negotiation. They're all the things that are difficult about adolescence. And adolescence is the time when people are using technology to skip and to cut corners and to not have to do some of these very hard things.[69]

Virtual encounters more often than not undermine authentic communication and minimize accountability, and I would say pose a significant challenge to the communal foundation of public values. As Turkle points out, digital technologies have become the new architect of our intimacies, but while the digital terrain offers the promise of new forms of sociality it more often than not delivers the scandal of empty emotional lives and "risk free" forms of sociality and intimacy. In this brave new world, privacy is sacrificed to the overreach of new digital surveillance systems, while a discourse limited to the vocabulary of privatization becomes the only mode of communication capable of understanding that valuable freedoms are being lost in the rush to an alleged digital democracy. When the public simply becomes a realm in which the language of the private exhibits itself, politics as a democratic force comes to an end.

The new media—embodied, for example, by the blogosphere—have enormous potential for enhancing public discourse by making power visible, articulating dissenting views, and bringing strangers and communities together, but that still provides no justification for neglecting on-the-ground social movements in which public spheres can develop their potential for real-time community engagement, in-person dialogue, and the collective mobilization of political pressure. Sally Kohn argues that "Internet activism is individualistic" and that "it does not bind individuals in shared struggle the same as face-to-face activism of the 1960s and 1970s did. It allows us to channel our individual power for good, but it stops there."[70] Angela Davis builds on this argument by claiming that we should not substitute virtual communities for "protracted struggles, protracted movements that require very careful organizing interventions that don't always depend on our capacity to mobilize demonstrations."[71] The Internet and diverse forms of social media are great for communicating to people and mobilizing demonstrations, as we have seen recently in the rising tide of worker and student protests in countries such as Iran, China, Syria, and Moldova,[72] but demonstrations cannot take the place of organized movements that need to be committed to the struggle for justice in the long haul.

There is an expanding list of complaints from users of the new media, especially with respect to young people, that ranges from the development of short attention spans, addiction to social networking, obsessions with video games, and damaged neurological functions to an overabundance of trivial information that seems to be spawning a growing anti-intellectualism or at the very least a general lack of thoughtfulness and discriminating judgment.[73] Although these problems are not unimportant, they are only part of the problem facing the crisis of public values in the age of the new digitally generated media. The equally concerning, if not more serious, problems, both political and educational, are about access to the landscape of technoculture and the creation of public spheres that can provide the ideas, knowledge, and values necessary to situate the new media within a more democratic set of ideals, values, and social relations. The struggle for reclaiming public values is in essence part of a larger strategy to create a new kind of subjectivity and social agency different from that produced within a neoliberal framework and market-driven mode of public pedagogy. The conditions for democracy do not come easily and must be struggled over continuously. Clearly, the new media can play a crucial role both for and against that struggle.

Where the liberatory possibilities of the next generation of media technologies become significant is in the efforts of individuals, groups, and institutions to deploy the pedagogical potential of the new media in constructing new knowledge, including new voices in the conversation, forging alliances across national boundaries, and protecting those public spheres where the formative culture necessary for creating educated and informed citizens can develop and flourish.[74] The production of such knowledge, alliances, and voices must be connected to the urgent call to revitalize the language of civic education and social responsibility as part of a broader discourse of political agency, civic literacy, and critical citizenship in a globalized world. Reclaiming the connection between the political and the ethical imagination as a pedagogical act might be one of the most crucial challenges in the twenty-first century facing those who believe that the new media offer the prospect of a new and powerful global public sphere for promoting justice, public values, and the promise of democracy.

If a culture of questioning, required for thinking beyond the narrow framing mechanisms of casino capitalism, militarism, and religious fundamentalism, does not come into play, it is conceivable that the new media will surrender their political and pedagogical potential to an emergent form of authoritarianism that will relinquish even its most dubious claims on democracy. If a renewed culture of civic engagement recognizes the necessity for situating the new information technologies within the intersection of the pedagogical and the political, the new media can be appropriated to challenge neoliberal modes of commodification, privatization, and anti-intellectualism. And as formative critical cultures develop, the new media provide opportunities to become not only a progressive force for democracy but also one of the primary educational tools for making progress sustainable.

Without an urgent reconsideration of the rise of the new media alongside the waning of public values in the current shaping of U.S. society, the crucial gains of the past that extend from the Civil Rights Movement to the antiwar movements of the 1960s will be lost, offering neither inspiration nor models of struggles that lay claim to and defend democratic values, relations, and institutions. If we are to address any viable notion of the new media along with the public values that give it substantive meaning, we must marshal the power of pedagogy and critical inquiry as part of a broader attempt to revitalize the conditions for individual and social agency, while simultaneously addressing the most basic problems now preventing the realization of social justice and global democracy. Public values matter. They must become part of any ongoing attempt to give meaning to the interconnections among the new media, non-commodified public spheres, a formative culture that nurtures a belief in the common good and the ethical imagination, and the individual and collective practices needed to uphold the promise of an aspiring democracy.

Notes

1. Tony Judt, *Ill Fares the Land* (New York: Penguin, 2010), 2.

2. Zygmunt Bauman, *The Individualized Society* (London: Polity Press, 2001), 55.

3. Walter Benjamin, *The Writer of Modern Life: Essays on Charles Baudelaire* (Cambridge, MA: Harvard University Press, 2006), 160.

4. A partial list of excellent sources on neoliberalism includes: Pierre Bourdieu, *Acts of Resistance: Against the Tyranny of the Market* (New York: The New Press, 1998); Pierre Bourdieu, "The Essence of Neoliberalism," *Le Monde Diplomatique*, December 1998, online at http://www.en.monde-diplomatique.fr/1998/12/08bourdieu; Zygmunt Bauman, *Work, Consumerism and the New Poor* (London: Polity Press, 1998); Noam Chomsky, *Profit over People: Neoliberalism and the Global Order* (New York: Seven Stories, 1999); Jean Comaroff and John L. Comaroff, *Millennial Capitalism and the Culture of Neoliberalism* (Durham, NC: Duke University Press, 2000); Anatole Anton, Milton Fisk, and Nancy Holmstrom, eds., *Not for Sale: In Defense of Public Goods* (Boulder, CO: Westview Press, 2000); Alain Touraine, *Beyond Neoliberalism* (London: Polity Press, 2001); Colin Leys, *Market Driven Politics* (London: Verso, 2001); Randy Martin, *Financialization of Daily Life* (Philadelphia, PA: Temple University Press, 2002); Ulrich Beck, *Individualization* (London: Sage, 2002); Doug Henwood, *After the New Economy* (New York: The New Press, 2003); Pierre Bourdieu, *Firing Back: Against the Tyranny of the Market 2*, trans. Loic Wacquant, (New York: The New Press, 2001);

Loic Wacquant, *Punishing the Poor* (Durham, NC: Duke University Press, 2009); David Harvey, *The New Imperialism* (New York: Oxford University Press, 2003); David Harvey, *A Brief History of Neoliberalism* (New York: Oxford University Press, 2005); Henry A. Giroux, *Against the Terror of Neoliberalism* (Boulder, CO: Paradigm Publishers, 2008); Jodi Dean, *Democracy and Other Neoliberal Fantasies* (Durham, NC: Duke University Press, 2009); and Juliet B. Schor, *Plenitude: The New Economics of True Wealth* (New York: Penguin, 2010).

5. Peter Whoriskey, "With Executive Pay, Rich Pull Away from Rest of America," *Washington Post*, June 18, 2011, online at http://www.washingtonpost.com/business/economy/with-executive-pay-rich-pull-away-from-rest-of-america/2011/06/13/AGKG9jaH_story.html

6. Michael Winship, "The Rich Are Different," *CounterPunch*, June 28, 2011, online at http://www.counterpunch.org/winship06282011.html.

7. Ibid.

8. This theme is taken up powerfully by a number of theorists. See C. Wright Mills, *The Sociological Imagination* (New York: Oxford University Press, 2000); Richard Sennett, *The Fall of Public Man* (New York: Norton, 1974); Zygmunt Bauman, *In Search of Politics* (Stanford, CA: Stanford University Press, 1999); and Henry A. Giroux, *Public Spaces, Private Lives* (Lanham, MD: Rowman and Littlefield, 2001).

9. Craig Calhoun, "Information Technology and the International Public Sphere," Douglas Schuler and Peter Day, eds., *Shaping the Network Society: The New Role of Society in Cyberspace* (Cambridge, MA: MIT Press, 2004), 241.

10. Cited in Peter Beilharz, *Zygmunt Bauman: Dialect of Modernity* (London: Sage, 2000), 158.

11. Jeffrey Sachs, "America's Deepening Moral Crisis," *The Guardian*, October 4, 2010, online at http://www.guardian.co.uk/commentisfree/belief/2010/oct/04/americas-deepening-moral-crisis.

12. Classic examples of this can be found in the work of Milton Friedman and the fictional accounts of Ayn Rand. It is a position endlessly reproduced in conservative foundations and institutes such as the American Enterprise Institute, Heritage Foundation, Hudson Institute, Manhattan Institute for Policy Research, and the Hoover Institute. One particularly influential book that shaped social policy along these lines is Charles Murray, *Losing Ground* (New York: Basic, 1994).

13. For an excellent analysis of such groups, see Chris Hedges, *American Fascists: The Christian Right and the War on America*

(New York: Free Press, 2008). See also Giroux, *Against the Terror of Neoliberalism.*

14. The best work on this subject has been done by Zygmunt Bauman: *Wasted Lives* (London: Polity Press, 2004) and *Consuming Life* (London: Polity Press, 2007).

15. Henry A. Giroux, *Youth in a Suspect Society: Democracy or Disposability?* (New York: Palgrave, 2009); Michelle Alexander, *The New Jim Crow: Mass Incarceration in the Age of Colorblindness* (New York: The New Press, 2010); and Mike Davis, *No One Is Illegal* (Chicago: Haymarket, 2006).

16. See Giroux, *Youth in a Suspect Society,* and Loic Wacquant, *Punishing the Poor: The Neoliberal Government of Social Insecurity* (Durham, NC: Duke University Press, 2009).

17. See, for instance, David DeGraw, "The Economic Elite Have Engendered an Extraordinary Coup, Threatening the Very Existence of the Middle Class," *AlterNet,* February 15, 2010, online at http://www.alternet.org/module/printversion/145667; and Godfrey Hodgson, *More Equal than Others: America from Nixon to the New Century* (Princeton, NJ: Princeton University Press, 2006).

18. On the pernicious effects of inequality on human life, public values, and democracy in general, see Judt, *Ill Fares the Land,* and Richard Wilkinson and Kate Pickett, *The Spirit Level: Why Equality Is Better for Everyone* (New York: Penguin, 2009).

19. MCT News Service, "3.6 Million Older Americans Living in Poverty," *Chicago Tribune,* November 2, 2009, online at http://www.chicagotribune.com/business/yourmoney/sns-200911020804mctnewsservbc-pfp-graymatters-nd52,0,3069729,print.story.

20. Chris Hedges, *Empire of Illusion* (Toronto: Knopf Canada, 2009), 117.

21. Zygmunt Bauman, *Liquid Times: Living in an Age of Uncertainty* (London: Polity Press, 2007), 28.

22. Zygmunt Bauman, *Liquid Modernity* (London: Polity Press, 2001), 14.

23. For a brilliant analysis of the effects of social inequality globally, see Zygmunt Bauman, *Collateral Damage: Social Inequalities in a Global Age* (London: Polity Press, 2011).

24. Eric Alterman, "Kabuki Democracy: Why a Progressive Presidency Is Impossible, for Now," *The Nation,* July 7, 2010, online at http://www.thenation.com/print/article/37165/kabuki-democracy-why-progressive-presidency-impossible-now.

25. John Clarke, "Governing the Social?" *Cultural Studies* 21:6 (November 2007): 837–846.

26. Ronald Reagan, "First Inaugural Address," *American Rhetoric,* January 30, 1981, online at http://www.americanrhetoric.com/speeches/ronaldreagandfirstinaugural.html.

27. For an excellent summary of the attack on social rights in North America, see Ed Broadbent, "The Rise and Fall of Economic and Social Rights: What Next?" *Canadian Centre for Policy Alternatives,* May 2010, online at http://www.policyalternatives.ca/sites/default/files/uploads/publications/reports/docs/Rise_and_Fall_of_Economic_and_Social_Rights.pdf.

28. Clarke, "Governing the Social?" 996.

29. On the rise of the punishing state as a central feature of neoliberalism, see Wacquant, *Punishing the Poor.*

30. Clarke, "Governing the Social?" 996–997.

31. Judt, *Ill Fares the Land,* 157.

32. Mills, *Sociological Imagination,* 5.

33. Bauman, *Individualized Society,* 4.

34. This term is taken from Zygmunt Bauman, quoted in Gerry McCarthy, "*The Social Edge* Interview: Zygmunt Bauman," *The Social Edge,* February 2007, online at http://www.thesocialedge.com/articles/gerrymccarthy/index1.shtml.

35. See, for example, Francis Fukuyama's notorious and influential support for neoliberalism in *The End of History and the Last Man* (New York: The New Press, 1992). Fukuyama, in light of the militarization and radicalization of neoconservatism during George W. Bush's presidency, has since revised his earlier thesis. See his defense of the liberal democracy against U.S. imperialism in the more recent *America at the Crossroads: Democracy, Power, and the Neoconservative Legacy* (New Haven, CT: Yale University Press, 2006).

36. Wendy Brown, *Regulating Aversion: Tolerance in the Age of Identity and Empire* (Princeton, NJ: Princeton University Press, 2006), 16.

37. Bauman, *Individualized Society,* 55.

38. Sheldon S. Wolin, *Democracy Incorporated: Managed Democracy and the Specter of Inverted Totalitarianism* (Princeton, NJ: Princeton University Press, 2008), 259–260.

39. Wolin, *Democracy Incorporated,* 260–261.

40. These issues are addressed in more detail in Jeffrey Di Leo, Walter Jacobs, and Amy Lee, "The Sites of Pedagogy," *Symploke* 10:1–2 (2002): 7–12.

41. Raymond Williams, "Preface to Second Edition," *Communications* (New York: Barnes and Noble, 1967), 15.

42. C. Wright Mills, "The Cultural Apparatus," *The Politics of Truth: Selected Writings of C. Wright Mills* (Oxford: Oxford University Press, 2008), 204.

43. Ibid.

44. Ibid.

45. Cornelius Castoriadis, "Democracy as Procedure and Democracy as Regime," *Constellations* 4:1 (1997): 10.

46. Cornelius Castoriadis, "The Nature and Value of Equity," *Philosophy, Politics, Autonomy: Essays in Political Philosophy* (New York: Oxford University Press, 1991), 140.

47. Cornelius Castoriadis, "The Problem of Democracy Today," *Democracy and Nature* 8 (April 1996): 20.

48. Cornelius Castoriadis, "The Greek Polis and the Creation of Democracy," *Philosophy, Politics, Autonomy: Essays in Political Philosophy* (New York: Oxford University Press, 1991), 118.

49. Judith Butler, *Frames of War: When Is Life Grievable?* (New York: Verso, 2009), 13–14.

50. Judt, *Ill Fares the Land,* 15, 18.

51. See Jacques Derrida, *Specters of Marx* (New York: Routledge, 1994). See also Ivan Zatz, "The Weight of Nightmares: Small Screens, Social Space and Representation in Contemporary Capitalism," *Situations* 1:1 (April 2005): 143–159.

52. Zygmunt Bauman, *Globalization: The Human Consequences* (New York: Columbia University Press, 1998), 82.

53. On this issue, see Roberto Mangabeira Unger and Cornel West, *The Future of American Progressivism* (Boston: Beacon, 1998).

54. Stanley Aronowitz, "Commentary," in Mark Poster, *The Information Subject* (Amsterdam: Gordon and Breach, 2001), 176.

55. Zygmunt Bauman has been addressing this theme for many years. See his most recent *The Art of Life* (London: Polity Press, 2008) and *Living on Borrowed Time: Conversations with Citlali Rovirosa-Madrazo* (Cambridge: Polity Press, 2010).

56. All of these ideas are worked out in detail in Bauman, *Consuming Life.*

57. Hedges, *Empire of Illusion,* 33.

58. For an interesting critique of the new media and the rise of illiteracy among young people, see Spotlight on Digital Media and Learning (MacArthur Foundation), "Kaiser Study: Kids 8 to 18 Spend More Than Seven Hours a Day with Media," January 21, 2010, online at http://spotlight.macfound.org/blog/entry/kaiser_study_kids_age_8_to_18_spend_more_than_seven_hours_a_day_with_media; and Madeleine Bunting, "From Buses to Blogs, a Pathological Individualism Is Poisoning Public Life," *The Guardian/UK,* January 28, 2008, online at http://www.guardian.co.uk/commentisfree/2008/jan/28/comment.society. See also Jaron Lanier, *You Are Not a Gadget* (New York: Knopf, 2010).

59. David Ottalini, "Students Addicted to Social Media—New UM Study," *University of Maryland,* April 21, 2010, online at http://www.newsdesk.umd.edu/sociss/release.cfm?ArticleID.

60. Chris Hedges, "The Information Super-Sewer," *TruthDig,* February 15, 2010, online at http://www.truthdig.com/report/item/the_information_super-sewer_20100214.

61. Malcolm Gladwell, "Small Change: Why the Revolution Will Not Be Tweeted," *The New Yorker*, October 4, 2010, 42, 44–49.

62. See Peter Day and Douglas Schuler, "Prospects for a New Public Sphere," in Peter Day and Douglas Schuler, ed., *Shaping the Network Society*, 353–375.

63. Sometimes the political forces affecting the new media are noted by scholars but are not taken seriously enough. For instance, little is said about the framing mechanisms of neoliberalism and how it uses the Internet and digital media in ways that far outstrip their use by progressive forces. The media networks that emerged out of Seattle offer a glimmer of hope, but do little to adequately measure the imbalance of forces driving the new media. See, for example, Henry Jenkins and David Thorburn, "Introduction: The Digital Revolution, the Informed Citizen, and the Culture of Democracy," in Henry Jenkins and David Thornburn, ed., *Democracy and the New Media* (Cambridge, MA: MIT Press, 2004), 1–17.

64. Calhoun, "Information Technology and the International Public Sphere," 237.

65. Ibid., 240.

66. Derrida, *Specters of Marx*, 169.

67. On the prison as a core political institution in U.S. society, see Wacquant, *Punishing the Poor*. On the culture of commitment lite, see Bauman, *The Art of Life*.

68. See, for instance, Christopher Mitchell and David Morris, "The Battle Is Raging for Control of the Internet—and Big Corporations May Come Out on the Losing Side," *AlterNet*, July 3, 2010, online at http://www.alternet.org/media/147267/the_battle_is_raging_for_control_of_the_internet_-_and_big_corporations_may_come_out_on_the_losing_side/?page=entire.

69. PBS, "Interview with Sherry Turkle," *Frontline PBS*, February 2, 2010, online at http://www.pbs.org/wgbh/pages/frontline/digitalnation/interviews/turkle.html. Her critique of the new media is fully developed in Sherry Turkle, *Alone Together: Why We Expect More from Technology and Less from Each Other* (New York: Basic Books, 2011).

70. Sally Kohn, "Real Change Happens Off-line," *Christian Science Monitor*, June 30, 2008, online at http://www.csmonitor.com/Commentary/Opinion/2008/0630/p09s01-coop.html.

71. Angela Y. Davis, *Abolition Democracy: Beyond Empire, Prisons, and Torture* (New York: Seven Stories, 2005), 128–129.

72. Ellen Barry, "Protests in Moldova Explode, with Help of Twitter," *New York Times*, April 8, 2010, online at http://www.nytimes.com/2009/04/08/world/europe/08moldova.html; David Barboza and Keith Bradsher, "In China, Labor Movement Enabled by Technology," *New York Times*, June 16, 2010, B1; Noam Cohen,

"Twitter on the Barricades: Six Lessons Learned," *New York Times*, June 21, 2010, WK4.

73. Some of these criticisms can be found in Aronowitz, "Commentary," in Poster, *The Information Subject*, 155–179; Hubert Guillaud, "What Is Implied by Living in a World of Flow," *TruthOut*, January 6, 2010, online at http://www. truthout.org/what-implied -living-a-world-flow56203; Stéphane Baillargeon, "Emerging from the Media Fog," *TruthOut*, January 11, 2010, online at http:// www.truthout.org/emerging-media-fog56702; PBS, "Interview with Sherry Turkle"; PBS, "Interview with Clifford Nass," *Frontline PBS*, February 2, 2010, online at http://www.pbs.org/wgbh/pages/ frontline/digitalnation/interviews/nass.html; and Hedges, "Information Super-Sewer."

74. See Richard Butsch, ed., *Media and Public Spheres* (New York: Palgrave, 2009).

◇

3

The Disappearing Intellectual in the Age of Economic Darwinism

> Not so long ago, the younger social scientist was apt to see his discipline as a vehicle for protest against society.... The seniors that set the fashion for him were frequently angry men ... and did not conceal strong opinions.... But this is now old hat: it is the 'bleeding-heart' school to the younger men ... they do not wish to protest; they wish to collaborate.
>
> —*William H. Whyte*[1]

We live at a time that might be appropriately called *the age of the disappearing intellectual*, a disappearance that marks with disgrace a particularly dangerous period in U.S. history. Although there are plenty of talking heads spewing lies, insults, and nonsense in the various media, it would be wrong to suggest that these right-wing populists are intellectuals. They are neither knowledgeable nor self-reflective, but largely ideological hacks catering to the worst impulses in U.S. society. Some obvious examples would include John Stossel calling for the repeal of that "section of the 1964 Civil Rights Act that bans discrimination in public places."[2] There is also MSNBC analyst Pat Buchanan who has called "Hitler an individual of great courage" and stated after Team USA's soccer loss against Mexico in July 2011 that "there are many Mexicans who may be U.S. citizens but are not truly Americans."[3] And, of course, there are the more famous corporate-owned talking heads, such as Charles Krauthammer, Michael

Savage, Bill O'Reilly, and Rush Limbaugh, all of whom trade in reactionary worldviews, ignorance, ideological travesties, racist tirades, and outlandish misrepresentations—all the while wrapping themselves in the populist creed of speaking for everyday Americans.

In a media scape and public sphere that views criticism, dialogue, and thoughtfulness as a liability, such anti-intellectuals abound, providing commentaries that are nativist, racist, reactionary, and morally repugnant. But the premium put on ignorance and the disdain for critical intellectuals is not monopolized by the dominant media; it appears to have become one of the few criteria left for largely wealthy individuals to qualify for public office. One typical example is Minnesota Congresswoman and Republican presidential candidate Michele Bachmann, who throws out inanities such as labeling the Obama administration a "gangster government."[4] She has claimed "that encouraging young people to be tolerant of gays is child abuse" ... and that "being gay is 'from Satan.'"[5] Or in a more vicious racist and historically incomprehensible vein, she has endorsed a document that states "Slavery had a disastrous impact on African American families, yet sadly a child born into slavery in 1860 was more likely to be raised by his mother and father in a two-parent household than was an African American baby born after the election of USA's first African American President."[6] Bachmann refuses to take critical questions from the press because she claims that they unfairly focus on her language. She has a point. After all, it might be difficult to support statements such as her claim that John Quincy Adams was one of the Founding Fathers (he was only nine when the Revolutionary War began); claiming falsely that President Obama released all of the oil from the strategic oil reserve; insisting that the founding fathers ended slavery even though many of them owned slaves, and so it goes.[7] When "Real Time" host Bill Maher asked Rep. Jack Kingston (R-GA) if he believed in evolution, Kingston answered by stating, "I believe I came from God, not from a monkey. If it happened over millions and millions of years, there should be lots of fossil evidence." Kingston did more than reject the modern foundation of evolutionary science, he also made it clear that he occupies a very special place on the stage of unqualified ignorance.[8] Kingston is more than confused about evolution, modern science, or the difference between evidence and empty opinions, he is also symptomatic of a right-wing political movement in the United States that embraces illiteracy and disdains logic, evidence, and facts. Another typical example can be found in Congressman Joe Barton's apology to BP for having to pay for damages to the government stemming from its disastrous oil spill.

This "upscaling of ignorance"[9] gets worse. Richard Cohen, writing in the *Washington Post* about Senator Michael Bennett, was shocked to discover that he was actually well-educated and smart but had to hide his qualifications in his primary campaign so as to not undermine his chance of being reelected. Cohen concludes that in politics, "We have come to value ignorance."[10] He further argues that the notion that a politician should actually know something about domestic and foreign affairs is now considered a liability:

> [W]e now have politicians who lack a child's knowledge of government. In Nevada, Sharron Angle has won the GOP Senate nomination espousing phasing out Social Security and repealing the income tax as well as abolishing that durable conservative target, the Education Department. Similarly, in Connecticut, Linda McMahon, a former pro wrestling tycoon, is running commercials so adamantly anti-Washington you would think she's an anarchist. In Arizona, Andy Goss, a Republican congressional candidate, suggests requiring all members of Congress to live in a barracks. This might be tough on wives, children and the odd cocker spaniel, but what the hell. Nowadays, all ideas are equal.[11]

The embrace of a type of rabid individualism, anti-intellectualism, persistent racism, and political illiteracy is also at work in the Tea Party movement. As social protections disappear, jobs are lost, uncertainty grows, and insecurity prevails, Tea Party members express disdain toward a weakened social state that represents one of the few institutions capable of providing the capital, policies, and safety nets necessary to protect those who have been shaken by the economic recession. And, yet, in light of what Bob Herbert calls "the most painful evidence imaginable of the failure of laissez-faire economics and the destructive force of the alliance of big business and government against the interests of ordinary Americans,"[12] the Tea Party movement wants to abolish government and expand even more the deregulated capitalism that has unsettled the lives of so many of its members. Ignorance prevails around both the movement's policy recommendations and its often racist protest against "the election of a 'foreign born'–African American to the presidency." As J. M. Bernstein pointed out in a *New York Times* opinion piece:

> When it comes to the Tea Party's concrete policy proposals, things get fuzzier and more contradictory: keep the government out of health care, but leave Medicare alone; balance the budget, but don't raise taxes; let individuals take care of themselves, but leave Social Security alone; and, of course, the paradoxical demand not to support Wall Street, to let the hard-working producers of wealth get on with it without regulation and government stimulus, but also to make sure the banks can lend to small businesses and responsible homeowners in a stable but growing economy.[13]

As the belief in the libertarian agent, free of all dependencies and social responsibilities, blows up in the face of the current economic meltdown, anger replaces critique, and ignorance informs politics. Bernstein thinks that members of the Tea Party are angry because they have been jolted into recognizing how fragile their so-called individual freedom actually is and that it is the government that is somehow responsible for making them feel so vulnerable. Maybe so, but there is also something else at work here, less metaphysical and more pedagogical—a kind of intellectual vacuum produced at different levels of U.S. society that cultivates ignorance, limits choices, legitimizes political illiteracy, and promotes violence. There is also a rigid ideological fundamentalism at work in this movement that wants to allow market-driven policies, practices, and values to determine every aspect of social, cultural, and political life, regardless of how destructive such forces are to the environment, youth, the elderly, workers, young families, and those who need social protections.

Another version of anti-intellectualism prevails in universities where students are urged by some conservative groups to spy on their professors to make sure they do not say anything that might actually get students to think critically about their beliefs. At the same time, faculty are being relegated to nontenured positions and because of the lack of tenure, which offers some guarantees, are afraid to say controversial things inside and outside the classroom for fear of being fired.[14] Moreover, as the university becomes more corporatized, intellectual and critical thought is transformed into a commodity to be sold to the highest bidder. I am not suggesting that so-called professed intellectuals are not influencing policy, appearing in the media, or teaching in the universities; however, these are not critical intellectuals. On the contrary, they are accommodating ideologues, content to bask in the politics of conformity and the rewards of official power. Underlying this drift toward the disappearing critical intellectual and the erasure of substantive critique is a regime of economic Darwinism in which a culture of ignorance serves to depoliticize the larger public while simultaneously producing individual and collective subjects necessary and willing to participate in their own oppression. The cheerful robot is not simply an opprobrium for ignorance—it is a metaphor for the systemic construction in U.S. society of a new mode of depoliticized thought and passive form of agency.

With the advent of neoliberalism, or what some call free-market fundamentalism, we have witnessed the production and widespread adoption throughout society of what I have called the politics of economic Darwinism. As a theater of cruelty and a mode of public pedagogy, economic Darwinism undermines all forms of solidarity while simultaneously promoting the logic of unrestricted individual responsibility. Yet, there is more at stake here than an unchecked ideology of privatization.[15] For example, as I mention throughout this book, the welfare state is being dismantled; it is being replaced by the harsh realities of the punishing state. Under such circumstances, social problems are increasingly criminalized and social protections are either eliminated or fatally weakened. The harsh values of this new social order can be seen in the increasing incarceration of young people, the modeling of public schools after prisons, the introduction of harsh anti-immigration laws, and state policies that bail out investment bankers but leave the middle and working classes in a state of poverty, despair, and insecurity. For poor youth of color and African American adults, the prison-industrial complex is particularly lethal. Michelle Alexander has pointed out that there are more African American men under the control of the criminal justice system than were enslaved in 1850 and that because of the war on drugs four out of five black youth in some communities can expect to be either in prison or "caught up in the criminal justice system at some point in their lives."[16] In states such as Georgia, Alabama, and South Carolina, new immigration laws "make it impossible for people without papers to live without fear. They give new powers to local police untrained in immigration law. They force businesses to purge workforces and schools to check students' immigration status. And they greatly increase the danger of unreasonable searches, false arrests, racial profiling, and other abuses, not just against immigrants, but anyone who may look like some officer's idea of an illegal immigrant.... The laws also make it illegal to give a ride to the undocumented, so a son could land in jail for driving his mother to the supermarket, or a church volunteer for ferrying families to a soup kitchen."[17] The Obama administration fares no better on punishing immigrants. In fact its stance on immigration suggests something about its own misplaced priorities. As Matt Taibbi has pointed out, law enforcement under the Obama regime has not convicted "a single executive who ran the companies that cooked up and cashed in on the phony financial boom."[18] And, yet, it has used its criminal justice system and law enforcement apparatus to deport 393,000 people, at a cost of $5 billion.[19] The Obama Administration has deported over 1 million immigrants.[20] White collar crooks cause global financial havoc because of their crooked deals and go scot-free while illegal immigrants looking for work that most Americans will not perform are put in jail. Welcome to America.

But the culture of cruelty, illegal legalities, and political illiteracy can also be seen in the practice of socialism for the rich. This is a practice in which government supports for the poor, unemployed, low-skilled workers, and elderly are derided because they either contribute to an increase in the growing deficit or undermine the market-driven notion of individual responsibility. And yet, the same critics defend without irony government support for the ultra-wealthy, the bankers, the permanent war economy, or any number of subsidies for corporations as essential to the life of the nation, which is simply an argument that benefits the rich and powerful and legitimizes the deregulated Wild West of casino capitalism. As public services are eliminated, health insurance is cut for more than a million kids, and teachers and public workers are laid off, corporate profits have soared and Wall Street executives are having a bonus year. The average worker in the United States made $752 a week for a total annual salary of $39,104 in 2010 and got a 0.5 percent pay increase, which amounted to $40,100.[21] According to the *New York Times*, "the median pay for top executives at 200 big companies last year was $10.8 million. That works out to a 23 percent gain from 2009."[22] The moral obscenity that characterizes such salaries becomes clear at a time when 14 million people are looking for work, 5.3 million are affected by the foreclosure epidemic, and thousands of families are trying to survive on food stamps. How can any society that calls itself democratic and egalitarian justify salaries that are so grotesquely high that it is difficult to imagine how such wealth can be spent? For example, how can anyone justify paying CEOs such as Philippe P. Dauman, the head of Viacom, $85 million in 2010? Or for that matter, the $32.9 million paid to Michael White of DirecTV?[23] The hidden order of politics and culture of cruelty comes into play when it is revealed that Mark G. Parker, the CEO of Nike, got $13.1 million in 2010 but cut 1,750 jobs, and Peter L. Lynch, the CEO of Winn-Dixie, got $5.3 million and eliminated 2,000 jobs. One of the worst offenders is Michael Duke, the CEO of Walmart, who got $18.7 million in pay in 2010 while cutting 13,000 jobs.[24]

What is daunting about all of these figures is that executive pay raises not only deepen inequality in the United States and result in the firing of workers in order to line the pockets of rich CEOs, but also concentrate enormous amounts of political, economic, and social power in the hands of a few individuals and corporations. In the end, such practices contribute to massive amounts of suffering on the part of millions of Americans; they corrupt politics; and undermine the promise of a viable democracy. Frank Rich expands this critique in arguing that "As good times roar back for corporate America, it's bad enough that CEOs are collectively sitting on some $1.9 trillion. America's total expenditure on the Iraq and Afghanistan wars over a decade has been $1.3 trillion. But what's most galling is how many of these executives are sore winners, crying all the way to Palm Beach while raking in record profits and paying some of the lowest tax rates over the past 50 years."[25]

Of course, this form of economic Darwinism is not enforced simply through the use of a government in the hands of right-wing corporate extremists, a conservative Supreme Court, or reliance upon the police and other repressive apparatuses; it is also endlessly reproduced through the cultural apparatuses of the new and old media, public and higher education, as well as through the thousands of messages and narratives we are exposed to daily in multiple commercial spheres. In this discourse, the economic order either is sanctioned by God or exists simply as an extension of nature. In other words, the tyranny and suffering that is produced through the neoliberal theater of cruelty are coded as unquestionable and unmovable as an urban skyscraper. Long-term investments are now replaced by short-term gains and profits, while at the same time compassion is viewed as a weakness and democratic public values are scorned because they subordinate market considerations to the common good. Morality in this instance becomes painless, stripped of any obligations to the other. As the language of privatization, deregulation, and commodification replaces the discourse of the public good, all things public, including public schools, libraries, and public services, are viewed either as a drain on the market or as a pathology. In addition, inequality in wealth and income expands, spreading like a toxin through everyday life, poisoning democracy and relegating more and more individuals to a growing army of disposable human waste.[26]

Illiteracy and moral responsibility thrive on the politics of the disconnect. For example, the giant oil spill in the Gulf of Mexico is rarely viewed as part of a much broader systemic crisis of democracy. Instead, it is treated as an unfortunate disaster caused by corporate greed or negligence. Widespread poverty is relegated to private anecdotes and rarely understood as part of the collateral damage inflicted by a harsh form of neoliberalism. The politics of the disconnect is reinforced by a banal entertainment state that views thinking as an impediment to happiness. Celebrity culture puts much of the population in a moral coma and perpetual state of ignorance. Coupled with a pedagogy of economic Darwinism that is spewed out daily in the mainstream media, large segments of the population are prevented from connecting the dots between their own personal troubles and larger social problems. In this case, the broader structural elements of a corrupt economic system disappear, while the suffering and hardship continues and the bankers and other members of the financial criminal class run to the banks to deposit their obscene bonuses.

Higher Education and the Public Relations Intellectual

Under such circumstances, to paraphrase C. W. Mills, we are seeing the breakdown of democracy, the disappearance of critical thought, and "the collapse of those public spheres which offer a sense of critical agency and social imagination."[27] Since the 1970s, we have witnessed the forces of market fundamentalism strip education of its public values, critical content, and civic responsibilities as part of its broader goal of creating new subjects wedded to the logic of privatization, efficiency, flexibility, consumerism, and the destruction of the social state. Tied largely to instrumental purposes and measurable paradigms, many institutions of higher education are now committed almost exclusively to economic growth, instrumental rationality, and preparing students for the workforce.

The question of what kind of education is needed for students to be informed and active citizens is rarely asked.[28] Hence, it not surprising, for example, to read that "Thomas College, a liberal arts college in Maine, advertises itself as Home of the Guaranteed Job!"[29] Faculty within this discourse are defined largely as a subaltern class of low-skilled entrepreneurs, removed from the powers of governance and subordinated to the policies, values, and practices within a market model of the university.[30] Within both higher education and the educational force of the broader cultural apparatus—with its networks of knowledge production in the old and new media—we are witnessing the emergence and dominance of powerful and ruthless, if not destructive, market-driven forms of governance, teaching, learning, freedom, agency, and responsibility. Such modes of education do not foster a sense of organized responsibility central to a democracy. Instead, they foster what might be called a sense of organized irresponsibility—a practice that underlies the economic Darwinism, public pedagogy, and corruption at the heart of both the current recession and U.S. politics.

The antidemocratic values that drive free-market fundamentalism are embodied in policies now attempting to shape diverse levels of higher education all over the globe. The script has now become overly familiar and more and more taken for granted, especially in the United States and increasingly in Canada. Public and higher education are now being shaped by a corporate-based ideology that embraces standardizing the curriculum, supporting top-down management, implementing more courses that promote business values, and reducing all levels of education to job training sites. For example, one university is offering a master's degree to students who commit to starting a high-tech company, and another allows career officers to teach capstone research seminars in the humanities. In one of these classes, the students were asked to "develop a 30-second commercial on their 'personal brand.'"[31]

The demise of democracy is now matched by the disappearance of vital public spheres and the exhaustion of intellectuals. Instead of critical and public intellectuals, faculty are increasingly defined less as intellectuals than as technicians, specialists, and grant writers. Nor is there any attempt to legitimize higher education as a fundamental sphere for creating the agents necessary for an aspiring democracy. In fact, the commitment to democracy is beleaguered, viewed less as a crucial educational investment than as a distraction that gets in the way of connecting knowledge and pedagogy to the production of material and human capital. In short, higher education is now being retooled as part of a larger political project to bring it in tune with the authority and values fostering the advance of neoliberalism. I think David Harvey is right in insisting that "the academy is being subjected to neoliberal disciplinary apparatuses of various kinds [while] also becoming a place where neoliberal ideas are being spread."[32]

As a core political and civic institution, higher education rarely appears committed to addressing important social problems. Instead, many colleges and universities have become unapologetic accomplices to corporate values and power and in doing so increasingly make social problems either irrelevant or invisible. Steeped in the same market-driven values that produced the 2008 global economic recession along with a vast amount of hardships and human suffering in many countries around the globe, higher education mimics the inequalities and hierarchies of power that inform the failed financial behemoths—banks and investment companies in particular—that have become public symbols of greed and corruption. Not only does neoliberalism undermine civic education and public values and confuse education with training, it also treats knowledge as a product, promoting a neoliberal logic that views schools as malls, students as consumers, and faculty as entrepreneurs. Just as democracy appears to be fading in the United States, so is the legacy of higher education's faith in and commitment to democracy. As the humanities and liberal arts are downsized, privatized, and commodified, higher education finds itself caught in the paradox of claiming to invest in the future of young people while offering them few intellectual, civic, and moral supports.

What is crucial to recognize is that higher education might be one of the few institutions we have left in the United States that provides the formative culture necessary to teach students the knowledge, values, and learning necessary for nurturing public values, critical hope, and a sense of civic responsibility. Students need to learn a great deal more than the narrow market values and practices that currently drive much of higher learning. They must learn how to think critically, understand the particular in light of the totality of larger relationships, develop a sense of social responsibility, and learn how to hold power accountable. Ian Angus is right in arguing that at "the core of the university is the encounter between students and faculty, and it is their responsibility to undertake that encounter in a spirit of enlightenment. Otherwise, what they do could be done better elsewhere. A community engaged in the search for knowledge enacts critical thinking. The justification for academic freedom lies in the activity of critical thinking. Genuine searching requires criticism of received truths and constituted powers and demands the mutual criticism of students and teachers based in the quality of their ideas rather than their social positions."[33] It is in precisely this sense of functioning as a democratic public sphere that higher education takes on a crucial and absolutely necessary public function.

It might be the case that everyday life is increasingly organized around market principles; but confusing a market-determined society with democracy hollows out the legacy of higher education, whose deepest roots are moral, not commercial. This is a particularly important insight, in a society where not only the free circulation of ideas is being replaced by ideas managed by the dominant media, but where critical ideas are increasingly viewed or dismissed as banal, if not reactionary.

But there is more at stake than simply the death of critical thought. There is also the powerful influence of celebrity culture and the commodification of culture, both of which now create a powerful form of mass illiteracy that increasingly dominates all aspects of the wider cultural educational apparatus. Yet mass illiteracy does more than undermine critical thought and depoliticize the public—it also becomes complicit with the suppression of dissent. Intellectuals who engage in dissent or a culture of questioning are often dismissed as irrelevant, extremist, or un-American.

Anti-public intellectuals now dominate the larger cultural landscape, funded largely by right-wing institutes, eager to legitimize the worst forms of oppression, as they nod, smile, speak in sound bites, and willingly display their brand of moral cowardice. At the same time, there are too few critical academics willing to defend higher education for its role in providing a supportive and sustainable culture in which a vibrant critical democracy can flourish.

As potential democratic public spheres, institutions of higher education are especially important at a time when any space that produces "critical thinkers capable of putting existing institutions into question" is under siege by powerful economic, military, and political interests.[34] The increasing disappearance of any viable public sphere, coupled with the reduction of the university to an outpost of business culture, represents a serious political and pedagogical concern that should not be lost on either academics or those concerned about the purpose and meaning of higher education, if not the fate of democracy itself.

Democracy places civic demands upon its citizens, and such demands point to the necessity of an education that is broad-based, critical, and supportive of meaningful civic values, participation in self-governance, and democratic leadership. Only through such a formative and critical educational culture can students learn how to become individual and social agents, rather than merely disengaged spectators, able to think otherwise and to act upon civic commitments that demand a rethinking and reordering of basic power arrangements fundamental to promoting the common good and producing a meaningful democracy. The current neoliberal regime that is wreaking havoc on the planet and the lives of millions cannot be addressed by future generations unless they have the capacities, knowledge, skills, and motivation to think critically and act courageously. This means giving them the knowledge and skills to make power visible and politics an important sphere of individual and collective struggle.

One measure of the degree to which higher education has lost its moral compass is obvious in the ways in which it disavows any relationship between equity and excellence, eschews the discourse of democracy, and reduces its commitment to learning to the stripped down goals of either preparing students for the workforce or teaching them the virtues of measurable utility. Although such objectives are not without merit, they have little to say about the role that higher education might play in influencing the fate of future citizens and the state of democracy itself, nor do they say much about what it means for faculty to be more than technicians or hermetic scholars.

In addition to promoting measurable skills and educating students to be competitive in the marketplace, academics are also required to speak a kind of truth, but as Stuart Hall points out, "maybe not truth with a capital *T*, but ... some kind of truth, the best truth they know or can discover [and] to speak that truth to power."[35] Implicit in Hall's statement is an awareness that to speak truth to power is not a temporary and unfortunate lapse into politics on the part of academics: It is central to opposing all those modes of ignorance, whether they are market-based or rooted in other fundamentalist ideologies that make judgments difficult and democracy dysfunctional.

In my view, academics have a moral and pedagogical responsibility not only to unsettle and oppose all orthodoxies and to make problematic the commonsense assumptions that often shape students' lives and their understanding of the world, but also to energize them to come to terms with their own power as individual and social agents. Higher education, in this instance, as Pierre Bourdieu, Paulo Freire, Stanley Aronowitz, and other intellectuals have reminded us, cannot be removed from the hard realities of those political, economic, and social forces that both support it and consistently, though in diverse ways, attempt to shape its sense of mission and purpose.[36] Politics is not alien to higher education but central to comprehending the institutional, economic, ideological, and social forces that give it meaning and direction. Politics also references the outgrowth of historical conflicts that mark higher education as an important site of struggle. Rather than the scourge of either education or academic research, politics is a primary register of their complex relation to matters of power, ideology, freedom, justice, and democracy.

Talking heads who proclaim that politics have no place in the classroom can, as Jacques Rancière points out, "look forward to the time when politics will be over and they can at last get on with political business undisturbed," especially as it pertains to the power-laden landscape of the university.[37] In this discourse, education as a fundamental basis for engaged citizenship, like politics itself, becomes a temporary irritant to be quickly removed from the hallowed halls of academia. In this stillborn conception of academic labor, faculty and students are scrubbed clean of any illusions about connecting what they learn to a world "strewn with ruin, waste and human suffering."[38]

As considerations of power, politics, critique, and social responsibility are removed from the university, the appeal to balance becomes code, as the famous sociologist C. Wright Mills points out, for "surface views which rest upon the homogeneous absence of imagination and the passive avoidance of reflection. A ... vague point of equilibrium between platitudes."[39] Under such circumstances, the university and the intellectuals that inhabit it disassociate higher education from larger public issues, remove themselves from the task of translating private troubles into social problems, and undermine the production of those public values that nourish a democracy. Needless to say, pedagogy is always political by virtue of the ways in which power is used to shape various elements of classroom identities, desires, values, and social relations, but that is different from being an act of indoctrination.

Writing about the role of the social sciences, Mills had a lot to say about public intellectuals in academia and in fact directly countered the argument that such intellectuals had no right to try to save the world:

> I do not believe that social science will "save the world" although I see nothing at all wrong with "trying to save the world"—a phrase which I take here to mean the avoidance of war and the re-arrangement of human affairs in accordance with the ideals of human freedom and reason. Such knowledge as I have leads me to embrace rather pessimistic estimates of the chances. But even if that is where we now stand, still we must ask: if there *are* any ways out of the crises of our period by means of intellect, is it not up to the social scientist to state them?... It is on the level of human awareness that virtually all solutions to the great problems must now lie.[40]

A large number of faculty exist in specialized academic bubbles, cut off from both the larger public and the important issues that impact society. Although extending the boundaries of specialized scholarship is important, it is no excuse for faculty to become complicit in the transformation of the university into an adjunct of corporate and military power. Too many academics have become incapable of defending higher education as a vital public sphere and unwilling to challenge those spheres of induced mass cultural illiteracy and firewalls of jargon that doom critically engaged thought, complex ideas, and serious writing for the public to extinction. Without their intervention as engaged intellectuals, the university defaults on its role as a democratic public sphere capable of educating an informed public, a culture of questioning, and the development of a critical formative culture connected to the need, as Cornelius Castoriadis puts it, "to create citizens who are critical thinkers capable of putting existing institutions into question so that democracy again becomes society's movement."[41]

Academics as Engaged Public Intellectuals

For education to be civic, critical, and democratic rather than privatized, militarized, and commodified, educators must take seriously John Dewey's notion that democracy is a "way of life" that must be constantly nurtured and defended.[42]

Democracy is not a marketable commodity and neither are the political, economic, and social conditions that make it possible.[43] If academics believe that the university is a space for and about democracy, they need to profess more, not less, about eliminating inequality in the university, supporting academic freedom, preventing the exploitation of faculty, supporting shared modes of governance, rejecting modes of research that devalue the public good, and refusing to treat students as merely consumers.

Academics have a distinct and unique obligation, if not political and ethical responsibility, to make learning relevant to the imperatives of a discipline, scholarly method, or research specialization. But more importantly, academics as engaged scholars can further the production of knowledge, passion, values, and hope in the service of forms of agency that are crucial to sustaining a democracy in which higher education plays an important civic, critical, and pedagogical role. If democracy is a way of life that demands a formative culture, educators can play a pivotal role in creating forms of pedagogy and research that enable young people to think critically, exercise judgment, engage in spirited debate, and create those public spaces that constitute "the very essence of political life."[44]

Economic Darwinism shapes more than economies; it also produces ideas, values, power, morality, and regimes of truth. Most importantly, regardless of its arrogance, it has to legitimize its power and theater of cruelty. Challenging its modes of legitimation and misrepresentations at the point of production is precisely an important task and mode of politics that should be addressed by all educators. Central ideological issues pushed by the advocates of neoliberalism, extending from the myth of free markets, free trade, the limitless power of individual agency, the evils of the welfare state, the necessity of low taxes, the economic benefits of a permanent war economy, deregulation, privatization, and commodification, along with the danger of giving the government any sense of public responsibility, should be challenged head-on in numerous venues by critical intellectuals.

As David Harvey points out, academics have a "crucial role to play in trying to resist the neoliberalization of the academy, which is largely about organizing within the academy ... creating spaces within the academy, where things could be said, written, discussed, and ideas promulgated. Right now those spaces are more under threat than they have been in many years."[45] All the more reason for academics to view the academy as a viable sphere worth struggling over. Intellectuals outside of the academy can also work to use their specific skills at various points of production to raise student consciousness and the level of public discourse in the spirit of creating agents capable of challenging and seeing beyond the existing neoliberal mode of economic Darwinism and other anti-democratic policies and practices. Such actions not only help intellectuals to be more self-reflective in creating effective critical public spheres, they also contribute to a formative culture of change that enables the development of a broad anti-capitalist movement.

What Harvey is rightfully suggesting is that academics can do more than "teach the conflicts" and provide the conditions that enable young people to speak truth to power. They can also organize within the academy to prevent the ongoing militarization and neoliberalization of higher education. They can work together with staff, students, part-time faculty, and other interested parties to form unions, embrace a notion of democratic governance, and help to position the university as a public sphere that can become a vital resource, in which people can think, engage in critical dialogue, organize, and connect to a broader public and to movements eager for economic and social transformation. Academics can work to develop diverse intellectual institutes, sites, and organizations, both within and outside of North America to contest the right-wing media machine and its army of anti-public intellectuals. Intellectuals trade in ideas, help to raise consciousness, and are crucial to offering new coordinates for how to think about freedom, justice, equality, sustainability, and the elimination of human suffering.

Jacques Rancière is informative here in his call for intellectuals to engage in a form of "dissensus," which he defines as an attempt to modify the coordinates of the visible and ways of perceiving experience. Dissensus is an attempt "to loosen the bonds that enclose spectacles within a form of visibility ... within the machine that makes the 'state of things' seem evident, unquestionable."[46] Ideas matter, not only because they can promote self-reflection, but because they can reconstitute our sense of agency, imagination, hope, and possibility. Intellectuals matter in such dark times. They not only have the ability to extend the reach and understanding of how ideas, power, and politics work, they can also offer a sense of hope while making clear the need for collective struggles so vital to deepening and expanding the possibilities of a sustainable democracy. As the commercial machinery and repressive apparatuses run by the neoliberal and right-wing zombies undermine public space and condemn more and more people to the status of disposable populations, it is all the more crucial that academics, artists, and other intellectuals mobilize their resources in order to fight the loss of vision and the exhaustion of politics that has paralyzed U.S. society for decades. As stated in the manifesto *Left Turn*, the key here is to "link struggles that have for decades been seen as discrete, with a broad anti-capitalist project whose objective is the radical transformation of economic, political, personal, and social relations."[47]

It is precisely over the creation of alternative democratic public spheres that such a struggle against neoliberal economic Darwinism can and should be waged by academics, intellectuals, artists, and other cultural workers. Higher education, labor unions, the alternative media, and progressive social movements offer important sites for intellectuals to form alliances, reach out to broader publics, and align with larger social movements. Critical intellectuals must do whatever they can to nurture formative critical cultures and social movements that can dream beyond the "mad-agency that is power in a new form, death-in-life."[48] At the same time, they must challenge all aspects of the neoliberal disciplinary apparatus—from its institutions of power to its pedagogical modes of rationality—in order to make its politics, pedagogy, and hidden registers of power visible. Only then will the struggle for the renewal of peace and justice become possible.

Notes

1. William H. Whyte, *The Organization Man* (New York: Simon and Schuster, 1956), 68.

2. Danila Perdomo, "Is John Stossel More Dangerous Than Glenn Beck?" *AlterNet*, July 3, 2010, online at www.alternet.org/story/147390/.

3. Patrick J. Buchanan, "Say Goodbye to Los Angeles," *CNSNEWS.com,* June 28, 2011, online at http://www.cnsnews .com/commentary/article/pat-buchanan-say-goodbye-los-angeles.

4. Michael Leahy, "Michele Bachmann Is Cool to Mainstream Media, and an Increasingly Hot Property," *Washington Post,* June 4, 2010, CO1.

5. Cited in Alexander Cockburn, "Pure Victims, Real Human Beings," *CounterPunch,* July 1–3, 2011, online at http://www .counterpunch.org/cockburn07012011.html.

6. Cheryl Contee, "Michele Bachmann Signs Pledge That Says Black Children Better Off During Slavery," *Jack and Jill Politics,* July 9, 2011, online at http://www.jackandjillpolitics .com/2011/07/michelle-bachmann-signs-pledge-that-says-black -children-better-off-during-slavery/.

7. See, for example, Lori Robertson, "Fact Checking Bach-mann," *FactCheck.Org,* June 16, 2011, online at http:// www.factcheck.org/2011/06/factchecking-bachmann/; Phil Thornton, "Fact-Checking Michele Bachmann: What Good Is It?" *Los Angeles Times,* January 27, 2011, online at http:// opinion.latimes.com/opinionla/2011/01/fact-checking-michele -bachmann-what-good-is-it.html; Tim Murphy, "Psycho Talk: The 32 Craziest Things GOP Presidential Contender Michele Bachmann Has Said," *AlterNet,* June 28, 2011, online at www.alternet.org/module/printversion/151439. See also Matt Taibbi, "Michele Bahmann's Holy War," *Rolling Stone,* June 7, 2011, online at http://www.rollingstone.com/politics/news/ michele-bachmanns-holy-war-20110622?page=1.

8. Steve Benen, "The Anti Science Party," *Washington Monthly,* January 29, 2011, online at http://www.washingtonmonthly .com/ archives/individual/2011_01/027759.php.

9. The term *upscaling of ignorance* was posted to my Facebook page by David Ayers.

10. Richard Cohen, "When Politics Goes Primitive," *Washington Post,* July 6, 2010, A13.

11. Ibid.

12. Bob Herbert, "When Greatness Slips Away," *New York Times,* June 21, 2010, online at http://www.nytimes.com/2010/06/22/ opinion/22herbert.html.

13. J. M. Bernstein, "The Very Angry Tea Party," *New York Times,* June 13, 2010, online at http://opinionator.blogs.nytimes .com/2010/06/13/the-very-angry-tea-party/?scp=1&sq=J.M. %20Bernstein&st=cse.

14. Robin Wilson, "Tenure, RIP: What the Vanishing Status Means for the Future of Higher Education," *The Chronicle of Higher Education,* July 4, 2010, online at http://chronicle.com/article/ Tenure-RIP/66114/?sid=at&utm_source=at&utm_medium=en.

15. Zygmunt Bauman, *The Art of Life* (London: Polity Press, 2008), 88.

16. Cited in Dick Price, "More Black Men Now in Prison System Than Were Enslaved," *LA Progressive,* March 31, 2011, online at http://www.zcommunications.org/more-black-men-now-in-prison -system-than-enslaved-in-1850-by-dick-price. See also Michelle Alexander, *The New Jim Crow: Mass Incarceration in the Age of Colorblindness* (New York: New Press, 2010).

17. Editorial, "It Gets Even Worse," *New York Times,* July 3, 2011, A16.

18. Matt Taibbi, "Why Isn't Wall Street in Jail?" *Rolling Stone,* February 16, 2011, online at http://www.rollingstone.com/politics /news/why-isnt-wall-street-in-jail-20110216.

19. Ibid.

20. Luis Gutierrez, "President Obama's Lost Pledge to Latinos," *The Guardian,* August 1, 2011, online at www.guardian.co.uk/ commentsfree/cifamerica/2011/aug/01/us-immigration-obama.

21. Pradnya Joshi, "We Knew They Got Raises. But This?" *New York Times,* July 2, 2011, BU1.

22. Ibid.

23. Ibid.

24. Josh Harkinson, "10 CEOs Who Got Rich by Squeezing Workers," *MotherJones,* May 12, 2011, online at http://motherjones .com/mojo/2011/05/ceo-executive-pay-layoffs.

25. Frank Rich, "Obama's Original Sin," *New York,* July 3, 2011, online at http://nymag.com/news/frank-rich/obama-economy/ presidents-failure/.

26. On the pernicious effects of inequality in U.S. society, see Tony Judt, *Ill Fares the Land* (New York: Penguin Press, 2010). Also see, Göran Therborn, "The Killing Fields of Inequality," *Open Democracy,* April 6, 2009, online at http://www.opendemocracy. net/article/the-killing-fields-of-inequality.

27. C. Wright Mills, *The Politics of Truth: Selected Writings of C. Wright Mills* (New York: Oxford University Press, 2008), 200.

28. Stanley Aronowitz, "Against Schooling: Education and Social Class," *Against Schooling* (Boulder, CO: Paradigm Publishers, 2008), xii.

29. Kate Zernike, "Making College 'Relevant,'" *New York Times,* January 3, 2010, ED16.

30. Although this critique has been made by many critics, it has also been made recently by the president of Harvard University. See Drew Gilpin Faust, "The University's Crisis of Purpose," *New York Times,* September 6, 2009, online at http://www.nytimes .com/2009/09/06/books/review/Faust-t.html.

31. Zernike, "Making College 'Relevant,'" ED16.

32. Harvey cited in Stephen Pender, "An Interview with David Harvey," *Studies in Social Justice* 1:1 (Winter 2007): 14.

33. Ian Angus, "Academic Freedom in the Corporate University," ed. Mark Cote, Richard J. F. Day, and Greig de Peuter, *Utopian Pedagogy: Radical Experiments against Neoliberal Globalization* (Toronto: University of Toronto Press, 2007), 67–68.

34. Cornelius Castoriadis, "Democracy as Procedure and Democracy as Regime," *Constellations* 4:1 (1997): 5.

35. Stuart Hall, "Epilogue: Through the Prism of an Intellectual Life," in Brian Meeks, *Culture, Politics, Race, and Diaspora: The Thought of Stuart Hall* (Miami, FL: Ian Rundle Publishers, 2007), 289–290.

36. See also Henry A. Giroux and Susan Searls Giroux, *Take Back Higher Education* (New York: Palgrave, 2004).

37. Jacques Rancière, *On the Shores of Politics* (London: Verso Press, 1995), 3.

38. Edward Said, *Humanism and Democratic Criticism* (New York: Columbia University Press, 2004), 50.

39. C. Wright Mills, "Culture and Politics: The Fourth Epoch," *The Politics of Truth: Selected Writings of C. Wright Mills* (New York: Oxford University Press, 2008), 199.

40. C. Wright Mills, "On Politics," *The Sociological Imagination* (New York: Oxford University Press, 2000), 193.

41. Cornelius Castoriadis, "Democracy as Procedure and Democracy as Regime," *Constellations* 4:1 (1997): 10.

42. See, especially, John Dewey, *The Public and Its Problems* (New York: Swallow Press, 1954).

43. John Keane, "Journalism and Democracy Across Borders," in Geneva Overholser and Kathleen Hall Jamieson, eds., *The Press: The Institutions of American Democracy* (New York: Oxford University Press, 2005), 92–114.

44. See, especially, H. Arendt, *The Origins of Totalitarianism*, 3rd edition, revised (New York: Harcourt Brace Jovanovich, 1968); and J. Dewey, *Liberalism and Social Action* [orig. 1935] (New York: Prometheus Press, 1999).

45. Cited in Pender, "An Interview with David Harvey," 14.

46. Fulvia Carnevale and John Kelsey, "Art of the Possible: An Interview with Jacques Rancière," *Artforum* (March 2007): 259–260.

47. Manifesto, *Left Turn: An Open Letter to U.S. Radicals* (New York: The Fifteenth Street Manifesto Group, March 2008), 6.

48. I have borrowed this phrase from my colleague David L. Clark.

◇

4

Living in the Age of Imposed Amnesia

The Eclipse of Democratic Formative Culture

We live in an age in which punitive justice and a theater of cruelty have become the defining elements of a mainstream cultural apparatus that trades in historical and social amnesia. How else to explain the 2010 congressional electoral sweep that put the most egregious Republican Party candidates back in power? These are the people who gave us Katrina, made torture a state policy, promoted "racial McCarthyism,"[1] celebrated immigrant bashing, pushed the country into two disastrous wars, built more prisons than schools, bankrupted the public treasury, celebrated ignorance over scientific evidence ("half of new Congressmen do not believe in global warming"[2]), and promoted the merging of corporate and political power. For the public to forget so quickly the legacy of the injustices, the widespread corruption, and the moral abyss created by this group (along with a select number of conservative democrats) points to serious issues with the pedagogical conditions and cultural apparatuses that made the return of the zombie politicians possible. The moral, political, and memory void that enabled this vengeful and punishing historical moment reached its shameful apogee by allowing the pathetic George W. Bush to reappear with a 44 percent popularity rating and a book tour touting his memoirs—the ultimate purpose of which is to erase any vestige of historical consciousness and make truth yet another casualty of the social amnesia that has come to characterize the U.S. century.

Imposed amnesia is the modus operandi of the current moment. Not only is historical memory now sacrificed to the spectacles of consumerism, celebrity culture, hyped-up violence, and a market-driven obsession with the self, but the very formative culture that makes compassion, justice, and an engaged citizenry foundational to democracy has been erased from the language of mainstream politics and the diverse cultural apparatuses that support it. Unbridled individualism along with the gospel of profit and unchecked competition undermine both the importance of democratic public spheres and the necessity for a language that talks about shared responsibilities, the public good, and the meaning of a just society. Politics is now defined through a language that divorces the ethical imagination from any sense of our ethical responsibilities. Even though it appears that neoliberalism has proven to be a death sentence on democracy, it becomes increasingly unimaginable for the American public to distinguish between market freedoms and political freedoms or to recognize the immense gap between formal rights and the ability to exercise such rights effectively.[3] Consequently, it becomes more and more difficult to connect politics with the importance of what I above refer to as the social question—with its emphasis on defining society in terms of public values, the common good, spiritual well-being, and "an imagined totality woven of reciprocal dependence, commitment and solidarity."[4]

Enforced forgetting subordinates public time to corporate time and eliminates those public spheres that might challenge it, especially in a society where business interests powerfully influence all existing socio-cultural-political institutions. Corporate time demands that we never stop moving—it is time organized around increased production, and it embodies a resistance to any space or mode of time that would allow us to think critically about how life might be reconfigured to expand and deepen a democratic polity. Against this notion of corporate time, with its construction of imposed forgetting, we need a language that embraces what might be called public time—a mode of time and space that resists the rapid-fire demand to keep moving, keep buying, and stop thinking. Public time is not driven by the necessity to consume or lose oneself in the never-ending spectacles of sound bite–driven talk shows, reality television, and celebrity culture. On the contrary, it registers a different understanding of time, rooted in the necessity to provide conditions in which people can slow down enough to be thoughtful, exercise informed judgments, and engage in social relations that affirm solidarity, the public good, and the need to struggle collectively to implement the promises of a democratic society. According to democratic theorist Cornelius Castoriadis, public time represents "the emergence of a dimension where the collectivity can inspect its own past as the result of *its own actions*, and where an indeterminate future opens up as a domain for its activities."[5] For Castoriadis, public time puts into question established institutions and dominant authority. Rather than maintaining a passive attitude toward power, public time demands and encourages forms of political agency based on a passion for self-governing, actions informed by critical judgment, and a commitment to linking social responsibility and social transformation. Public time legitimates those pedagogical practices that provide the basis for a culture of questioning, one that furthers the knowledge, skills, and social practices that encourage an opportunity for resistance, a space of translation, and a proliferation of discourses. Public time unsettles common sense and disturbs authority while encouraging critical and responsible leadership.

As Roger Simon observes, public time "presents the question of the social—not as a space for the articulation of pre-formed visions through which to mobilize action, but as the movement in which the very question of the possibility of democracy becomes the frame within which a necessary radical learning (and questioning) is enabled."[6] Public time affirms a politics without guarantees and a notion of the social that is open and contingent. It provides a conception of democracy that is never complete and determinate but constantly open to different understandings of the contingency of its decisions, mechanisms of exclusion, and operations of power.[7] At its best, public time renders governmental power explicit, and in so doing it rejects the language of ritualistic adherence and the abrogation of the conditions necessary for the assumption of basic rights and freedoms.

Moreover, public time considers civic education the basis, if not essential dimension, of justice, because it provides the conditions for individuals to develop the skills, knowledge, and passions to talk back to power while simultaneously constructing forms of political agency that encourage modes of social responsibility through active participation in the very process of governing.

Democracy, in part, can be measured by the smoothness in which private troubles can be translated into larger social issues and vice versa. The precondition for such translations are those educational spaces in which time is not instrumentalized but slowed down and made available for individuals to speak, deliberate, learn, engage in critical dialogues, and develop the habits of self- and social reflexivity. If public time is crucial to creating democratic citizens, the formative culture that provides the pedagogical practices and public spheres that make public time possible as an essential condition for democracy must be incorporated into any serious notion of public values and politics. The waning of democratic public values and meaningful spirituality has become a serious crisis confronting U.S. politics. Although public values have been in tension with dominant economic, political, and social forces for decades, the notion of the common good seems no longer capable of mobilizing a polity against the impassioned attacks of right-wing forces that now dominate political and cultural life in the United States. The neoliberal fervor for unbridled individualism, the disdain for community and the social state, and the expressed hatred for the public good—readily identified by the right as pathological—have produced "a weakening of democratic pressures, a growing inability to act politically, [and] a massive exit from democratic politics and from responsible citizenship."[8]

What is "disturbing" about the undermining of public values in U.S. society is that they have become irrelevant to the existing contemporary neoliberal order, which saps the foundation of social solidarity, weakens the bonds of social obligation, and insists on the ability of markets to solve all social and individual problems.[9] In light of the recent spectacle of a right-wing fringe being treated by the media as respectable politicians riding the wave of the Tea Party movement, many progressives have pointed to the emergent shadow of authoritarianism that is overtaking the country.[10]

Surely, they are on to something important, but what they rarely do is talk about the formative culture that transforms genuine anger and political concerns into a right-wing political movement. Although focusing criticism on the looniest personalities in this group—whether it be Sarah Palin, Michele Bachmann, or Chris Christie—might offer some political capital and a certain amount of catharsis, the real focus should be on those pedagogical forces at work in U.S. culture that allow these candidates to resonate so powerfully with the needs of people who are largely oppressed by the policies these candidates endorse. Noam Chomsky is entirely right in stating that, "Ridiculing Tea Party shenanigans is a serious error, however. It is far more appropriate to understand what lies behind the movement's popular appeal, and to ask ourselves why justly angry people are being mobilized by the extreme right and not by the kind of constructive activism that rose during the Depression, like the CIO (Congress of Industrial Organizations)."[11]

Any understanding of why popular needs are being mobilized by the right can only become productive if we illuminate how the educational force of the wider culture works to define, incorporate, and colonize such needs. We need to focus attention on how, to quote Fritz Stern, popular "resentment against a disenchanted secular world [finds] deliverance in the ecstatic escape of unreason."[12] This is not merely a political question but an important pedagogical one. Borrowing an insight from the great sociologist C. Wright Mills, the question to be posed is, How does the cultural apparatus in the United States function so powerfully and persuasively to connect the needs of so many Americans with the swindle of fulfillment offered by the ideologies of the extreme right? There is more at stake here than focusing on crass political ads. We need to understand better how conservative think tanks shape public opinion and policy; how the diverse sites of the old and new media reinforce a reactionary notion of common sense; and how market-driven values get normalized by erasing any viable understanding of history, memory, power, ideology, and politics.

I am fearful that the U.S. public and political systems are at a treacherous and perhaps irreversible point in history. The oligarchies of corporate and military power exhibit a deep disdain for democracy, and the public seems increasingly aware that their interests are being unmet and routinely dishonored. The disastrous effects of the choices made by the rich and powerful are painfully visible to the vast majority of people in the United States. Wall Street bankers and hedge fund managers rake in huge bonuses and exhibit an arrogance matched only by a contempt for those suffering under the weight of the current economic crisis. The financial elite scorn the social costs of their actions; they focus on an unflagging desire to make a profit at any expense. The new global elite no longer have any allegiance to the nation-state, its people, or its cultures. Negative globalization has made local politics irrelevant as financial power now travels unhampered by the boundaries or obligations of nation-states. The flight from political accountability and state regulation has been matched by the flight from moral, social, and political responsibility on the part of the rich and powerful. If progressives, radical social movements, religious institutions, and major unions don't address these issues as crucial pedagogical concerns and build the cultural apparatuses to challenge them, I fear that any vestige of democratic politics and knowledge will further disappear, and populist resentment will be almost completely harnessed to a pedagogical and political project that ironically restores class power to the mega-rich.[13]

With 17 million Americans unemployed, 5.3 million losing their homes, and more than 51 million without health insurance, people are desperate for jobs, mortgage relief, and health care they can afford. Without the necessary formative culture that can provide Americans with a language that enables them to recognize the political, economic, and social causes of their problems, a politics of despair, anger, and dissatisfaction can easily be channeled into a politics of violence, vengeance, and corruption, feeding far right-wing movements willing to trade in bigotry, thuggery, and brutality. We have already seen this happening with protests in London and other European cities. As the corporate state shreds all of the nation's social protections, it will take on the form of a punishing state and become more than willing to impose harsh disciplinary measures on those populations now considered disposable. The result will be a form of authoritarianism that brings about the utter collapse of democracy as a collective aspiration.

Recognizing how the social is being subordinated to market-driven interests points to the need to create new public spaces and the vocabulary for a politics in which a plurality of public spheres can promote, express, and create the shared values necessary to a thriving democracy. Reclaiming the social as part of a democratic imaginary entails making historical memory and the learning process central not simply to social change but to the struggle to democratize the very character of U.S. politics, institutional power, and public discourse. We see evidence of this attempt to reclaim a democratic imaginary in the profoundly important work done by Michael Lerner at *Tikkun,* Chris Hedges in his columns for *Truthdig,* Noam Chomsky's various interventions, Bill Moyers's legacy of critical journalism, Amy Goodman's important work for *Democracy Now,* and in independent online media such as *Truthout.* We need to rally behind and support the public intellectuals, media outlets, and growing social movements that are instrumental not only in providing the memory work needed to keep democracy alive but also in developing the conditions for a vibrant formative culture to provide alternative values, knowledge, social relations, and hope in the darkest of times.

Notes

1. This term comes from William Greider, "Obama without Tears," *The Nation,* November 10, 2010, online at http://www.thenation.com/article/156384/obama-without-tears.

2. Sarah Seltzer, "16 of the Dumbest Things Americans Believe—And the Right-Wing Lies Behind Them," *AlterNet,* November 13, 2010, online at http://www.alternet.org/story/148826/.

3. Zygmunt Bauman,*Collateral Damage: Social Inequalities in a Global Age* (London: Polity, 2011), 3.

4. Tony Judt, *Ill Fares the Land* (New York: Penguin, 2010); Zygmunt Bauman, "Has the Future a Left?" *Soundings* 35 (Spring 2007), online at http://www.lwbooks.co.uk/journals/articles/bauman07.html.

5. Cornelius Castoriadis, "The Greek Polis and the Creation of Democracy," *Philosophy, Politics, Autonomy: Essays in Political Philosophy* (New York: Oxford University Press, 1991), 113–114.

6. Roger I. Simon, "On Public Time," Ontario Institute for Studies in Education. Unpublished paper, April 1, 2002, 4.

7. Simon Critchley, "Ethics, Politics, and Radical Democracy—The History of a Disagreement," *Culture Machine,* online at http://www.culturemachine.tees.ac.uk/frm_f1.htm.

8. Zygmunt Bauman, *The Individualized Society* (London: Polity Press, 2001), 55.

9. A partial list of excellent sources on neoliberalism includes: Pierre Bourdieu, *Acts of Resistance: Against the Tyranny of the Market* (New York: The New Press, 1998); Pierre Bourdieu, "The Essence of Neoliberalism," *Le Monde Diplomatique,* December 1998, online at http://www.en.monde-diplomatique.fr/1998/12/08bourdieu; Zygmunt Bauman, *Work, Consumerism and the New Poor* (London: Polity Press, 1998); Noam Chomsky, *Profit over People: Neoliberalism and the Global Order* (New York: Seven Stories, 1999); Jean Comaroff and John L. Comaroff, *Millennial Capitalism and the Culture of Neoliberalism* (Durham, NC: Duke University Press, 2000); Anatole Anton, Milton Fisk, and Nancy Holmstrom, eds., *Not for Sale: In Defense of Public Goods* (Boulder, CO: Westview Press, 2000); Alain Touraine, *Beyond Neoliberalism* (London: Polity Press, 2001); Colin Leys, *Market Driven Politics* (London: Verso, 2001); Randy Martin, *Financialization of Daily Life* (Philadelphia: Temple University Press, 2002); Ulrich Beck, *Individualization* (London: Sage, 2002); Doug Henwood, *After the New Economy* (New York: The New Press, 2003); Pierre Bourdieu, *Firing Back: Against the Tyranny of the Market 2,* trans. Loic Wacquant (New York: The New Press, 2003); David Harvey, *The New Imperialism* (New York: Oxford University Press, 2003); David Harvey, *A Brief History of Neoliberalism* (New York: Oxford University Press, 2005); Henry A. Giroux, *Against the Terror of Neoliberalism* (Boulder, CO: Paradigm Publishers, 2008); Jodi Dean, *Democracy and Other Neoliberal Fantasies* (Durham, NC: Duke University Press, 2009); Juliet B. Schor, *Plenitude: The New Economics of True Wealth* (New York: Penguin, 2010); and Kean Birch and Vlad Mykhenko, *The Rise and Fall of Neoliberal-Liberalism* (New York: Zed Books, 2010).

10. I take up the issue of the emerging authoritarianism in the United States in *Against the Terror of Neoliberalism* (Boulder, CO: Paradigm Publications, 2008).

11. Noam Chomsky, "Outrage, Misguided," *In These Times,* November 4, 2010, online at http://www.inthesetimes.com/article/6615/outrage_misguided/.

12. Stern cited in Chomsky, "Outrage, Misguided."

13. David Harvey, *A Brief History of Neoliberalism* (New York: Oxford University Press, 2005).

◇

5

Defending Higher Education
as a Public Good

> If the university does not take seriously and rigorously its role as a guardian of wider civic freedoms, as interrogator of more and more complex ethical problems, as servant and preserver of deeper democratic practices, then some other regime or menage of regimes will do it for us, in spite of us, and without us.
>
> —*Toni Morrison*[1]

No doubt it will take some of us time to recover from the confident delusion that the global economic recession of 2008 would reveal once and for all the destructive force of neoliberalization, the "vampiric octopus" masquerading as free market efficiency and neutrality. But once again citizens in the overdeveloped West find themselves puzzling over stories of billion dollar bonuses for the very business "leaders" who were responsible for the meltdown—an inky black trail of endless zeros from whence red ink once bled out of the gaping wound of an impaled public trust. Even worse is the fact that the Obama administration has given a free pass to those responsible "for the greed and misdeeds that brought America to its gravest financial crisis since the Great depression."[2] No moral, legal, or financial reckoning for the Wall Street and financial industry gangsters responsible for the financial crisis of 2008. This was a crisis that, as Matt Taibbi puts it, "saw virtually every major bank and financial company on Wall Street embroiled in obscene criminal scandals that impoverished millions and collectively destroyed hundreds of billions, in fact trillions, of dollars of the world's wealth—and nobody went to jail."[3] Four decades of neoliberal social and economic policy has strangulated not only the middle class and the poor, but those social institutions organized in large part for their protection—an assault seen most aggressively at all levels of education in the United States. The consequence has been an entrenched political illiteracy (among other forms of illiteracy) across the electorate, which has fueled populist rage and provided an additional political bonus for those who engineered massive levels of inequality, poverty, and sundry other hardships. As social protections are dismantled, public servants are denigrated, and public goods such as schools, bridges, health care services, and public transportation deteriorate, the Obama administration unapologetically embraces the values of economic Darwinism and rewards its chief beneficiaries: mega banks and big business. Neoliberalism—reinvigorated by the passing of tax cuts for the ultrarich, the right-wing Republican Party taking over of the House of Representatives, and an ongoing successful attack on the welfare state—proceeds once again in zombie-like fashion to impose its values, social relations, and forms of social death upon all aspects of civic life.[4]

With its relentless attempts to normalize the irrational belief in the ability of markets to solve all social problems, neoliberal market fundamentalism puts in place policies designed to dismantle the few remaining vestiges of the social state, public spheres, and vital public services. More profoundly, it has weakened if not nearly destroyed those institutions that enable the production of a formative culture in which individuals learn to think critically, imagine other ways of being and doing, and connect their personal troubles with public concerns. Matters of justice, ethics, and equality have once again been exiled to the margins of politics. This is not to suggest that morality does not come into play under the regime of neoliberalism. Morality in neoliberal speak acts for the most part as a legitimating and shaming device. Fueled by a discourse of austerity, personal responsibility becomes the only morality that counts, as social and economic problems are deemed the result of individual failings. As morality is stripped of its social registers, it appears in the privatized discourse of family values and individual responsibility. The most vulnerable are now blamed for not sacrificing enough or are viewed with disdain because they argue for social protections, new infrastructures of sociality, and a new democratic imaginary. Disengagement has become the defining characteristic of neoliberal relations, and one consequence, as Zygmunt Bauman insists, is that, "just as we as individuals feel no responsibility towards the other, so does the sense of political responsibility for social problems weaken."[5] Anyone who does not adhere to the ideology of individual entrepreneurialism and unchecked narcissism is now viewed with disdain, if not contempt. Never has this assault on the democratic polity and public values been more obvious, if not more dangerous, than at the current moment, when a battle is being waged under the rubric of neoliberal austerity measures on the autonomy of academic labor, the classroom as a site of critical pedagogy, the rights of students to high-quality education, the democratic vitality of the university as a public sphere, and the role played by the liberal arts and humanities in fostering an educational culture that is about the practice of freedom and mutual empowerment.[6]

Although higher education has a long history of being attacked by various religious, political, and corporate forces, there is something unique about the current assault on the university.[7] At various points in the past, such as during the McCarthy era, individual professors were assailed for their political beliefs and affiliations.[8] During the 1980s and 1990s, progressive academics were initially targeted for their critical views toward the canon and for allegedly indoctrinating students.[9] They were seen as a threat by various right-wing ideologues and corporate groups who never forgot the challenge posed by student radicals of the 1960s to the increasing corporatization and militarization of the university.[10] Although the relationship of the university to corporate power and the warfare state was never far removed from the workings of the university, its hidden order of politics was partially offset by a democratic legacy, a set of liberal ideals, and a commitment to public values that strongly resonated with the United States's claim on the principles of democracy.[11] The institutional setting provided a space for the nurturing of democratic ideals and offered both a shelter for radical intellectuals and a mode of critique that vigorously defended higher education's public role and the formative culture and modes of literacy that were essential to its survival and promise.[12] Such a democratic mandate for the university, however compromised at times, was emboldened by various struggles for racial, gender, economic, and social justice in the second half of the twentieth century. The formative culture that made such struggles possible offered more than opportunities for political alignments. It also reinforced the long-standing view of the university as a democratic public sphere. Within such a sphere, critique, dialogue, critical theory, and informed judgment constituted a pedagogical necessity through which the institution could develop a public awareness of itself and empower administrators, researchers, teachers, and students to act in socially responsible ways that made such an awareness meaningful to those both inside and outside of the university.

As a result of this enduring, though tarnished, historical narrative, the democratic expression of pedagogical diversity and the political nature of education were viewed by many members of the U.S. public and intellectual classes as central not only to the civic mission of the university, especially the humanities and liberal arts, but also to the functioning of a just and democratic society. We are reminded of this legacy in recent times by Jacques Derrida's Enlightenment notion of the university as a place to think, to ask questions, and to exercise the autonomy necessary to both challenge authority and make it accountable.[13] Under the onslaught of a merciless economic Darwinism and theater of cruelty that has emerged since the 1980s, the historical legacy of the university as vital public good no longer fits into a revamped discourse of progress in which the end goal is narrowed to individual survival rather than the betterment of society as a whole. In fact, the concept of social progress has all but disappeared amid the ideological discourse of a crude market-driven presentism that has a proclivity for instant gratification, consumption, and immediate financial gain. If dissident professors were the subject of right-wing attacks in the past, the range and extent of the attack on higher education has widened and as a result become more dangerous. As Ellen Schrecker succinctly notes:

Today the entire enterprise of higher education, not just its dissident professors, is under attack, both internally and externally. The financial challenges are obvious, as are the political ones. Less obvious, however, are the structural changes that have transformed the very nature of American higher education. In reacting to the economic insecurities of the past forty years, the nation's colleges and universities have adopted corporate practices that degrade undergraduate instruction, marginalize faculty members, and threaten the very mission of the academy as an institution devoted to the common good.[14]

Memories of the university as a citadel of democratic learning have been replaced by a university eager to define itself largely in economic terms. For instance, Florida State University created two economics professorships through a $1.5 million gift from the conservative Koch brothers. In exchange for the gift, the university gave the Koch Foundation some say in the hiring of faculty. More specifically, the Koch Foundation can veto a hire paid for with their funds. Daniel Denvir points out that (conservative) Banker John Allison, longtime head of BB&T, has donated to 60 universities in exchange for their agreeing to teach Ayn Rand's *Atlas Shrugged*—some agreements even include the outrageous stipulation that the professor teaching the course "have a positive interest in and be well versed in Objectivism."[15] It gets worse.

At Texas A&M University, faculty evaluations are based on three key pieces of information: "their salary, how much external research funding they received and how much money they generated from teaching."[16] According to university administrators, "The information will allow officials to add the funds generated by a faculty member for teaching and research and subtract that sum from the faculty member's salary."[17] Besides being an insidious cost-cutting measure, this entrepreneurial logic dictates that a faculty member's performance is solely measured by their capacity to generate wealth for the university relative to their salary. Surely, this type of thinking could only be hatched in some conservative think tank eager to relegate all faculty to the status of Walmart workers. What is clear in this hyperrational calculus is that quantity compensates for quality and pedagogy is freed from any notion of ethical and social responsibility.

Frank Ashley, the vice chancellor for academic affairs at Texas A&M justifies this conservative and corporate accountability model on the grounds that it proves to the people of Texas that academia "pull[s] its weight."[18] Chancellor Michael D. McKinney also relies on a consumerist approach by measuring good classroom teaching according to student satisfaction. McKinney rewards faculty by offering a $10,000 bonus to teachers who get the highest student evaluations. He justifies the approach by stating, "This is customer satisfaction.... It has to do with students having the opportunity to recognize good teachers and reward them with some money."[19] And, yet, the research is abundantly clear in concluding that student evaluations are unreliable indicators of teacher performance. Such an approach does no more than reinforce a neoliberal notion of students as customers paying for a service, while turning faculty teaching into a form of entertainment that plays to what Cary Nelson, the president of the American Association of University Professors, calls "the applause meter."[20] Within this framework of simply giving students what they want, the notion of effective teaching as that which challenges commonsense assumptions and provokes independent, critical thought in ways that might be unsettling for some students as well as requiring from them hard work and introspection is completely undermined. Market-driven rewards cancel out the ethical imagination, social responsibility, and the pedagogical imperative of truth telling in favor of pandering to the predatory impulses behind narrow-minded individual awards and satisfactions. This is the self-deception, if not pedagogy, of scoundrels.

As the center of gravity shifts away from the humanities and the notion of the university as a public good, university presidents ignore public values while refusing to address major social issues and problems.[21] Instead, such administrators now display corporate affiliations like a badge of honor, sit on corporate boards, and pull in huge salaries. Until recently, Ruth Simmons, the president of Brown University sat on the board of Goldman Sachs and in 2009 earned $323,539 from the directorship and received a total of approximately $4.3 million in stock grants and options while serving on the board.[22] And she is not alone. A survey conducted by *The Chronicle of Higher Education* reported that "19 out of 40 presidents from the top 40 research universities sat on at least one company board."[23] Rather than treated as a social investment in the future, students are now viewed by university administrators as a major source of revenue for banks and other financial institutions that provide funds for them to meet escalating tuition payments. For older generations, higher education opened up opportunities for self-discovery as well as pursuing a career in the field of one's choosing. It was relatively cheap, rigorous, and accessible, even to many working-class youth. But as recent events in both the United States and Britain make clear, this is no longer the case. Instead of embodying the hope of a better life and future, higher education has become prohibitively expensive and exclusionary, now offering primarily a credential and for most students a lifetime of debt payments. Preparing the best and the brightest has given way to preparing what might be called Generation Debt.[24]

As the alleged Golden Age of higher education is mortgaged off to market-based values and instrumentalist modes of rationality, communal loyalties, deep-seated solidarities, and long-term commitments are sacrificed to private interests, individual life pursuits, and the new order of egoism.[25] As Sheldon Wolin has insightfully pointed out, the ideal of public commitment and the public spheres that sustain it have now become lost to history, fractured like public time itself by the frenetic speed at which financial transactions are exchanged, information is consumed, commitments are dissolved, and marginalized subjects are rendered disposable. Historical amnesia now works in tandem with the accelerated pace of capital to loosen the connection between higher education and public values, and with it the connection between pedagogy as a moral and political practice and the formative culture necessary for substantive democracy.[26] Memory and loss now make an urgent claim upon theory to assert that which "survives of the defeated, the indigestible, the unassimilated, the 'cross grained,' [and] the now wholly obsolete" and to become one of the few terrains left to imagine higher education beyond the corporate and militaristic logic of contemporary neoliberal values, politics, and modes of governance.[27]

As I have emphasized throughout this book, for the last three decades, we have witnessed in the United States the resurgence of a neoliberal disciplinary apparatus that has attempted to eradicate the social state, the concept of the public good, and any trace of the social contract. The obligations of citizenship have been replaced by the demands of consumerism, education has been reduced to another market-driven sphere, pedagogy has been instrumentalized, and public values have been transformed into private interests. Market-driven values, culture, and pedagogy offer up a new understanding of the citizen as a consumer, the university as hostage to the imperatives of business culture, and academic labor as a new subaltern class engaged in the production of the next generation of neoliberal subjects. At the same time, we have witnessed the substitution of political sovereignty by economic sovereignty and the replacement of the social state with a punishing state defined by a survival-of-the-fittest ethic that legitimates a form of economic Darwinism in which individuals now bear sole responsibility for their hardships, regardless of whether such forces are out of their reach and out of their control. As public issues collapse into private concerns, it becomes increasingly difficult to engage what C. Wright Mills called "the sociological imagination," defined as the ability to relate individual actions to larger historical and relational totalities, to connect private issues to broader public considerations.[28] Under such circumstances, not only is the power of dissent depoliticized and weakened, but those institutions and modes of thinking that embrace public values, democratic modes of critique, and a commitment to social justice and social responsibility are either defined as nostalgic reminders of the past or viewed as dangerous threats to a market society that considers itself synonymous with democracy. Those modes of agency that might be used for structural change, for rejecting the fetishism of the market and reimagining social relations not tied to the obligations of consumerism and hyper-individualism, now appear increasingly out of place in the current historical moment. Of course more than the power of dissent and public values is at risk. As Zygmunt Bauman argues, "The degree of democracy of a political regime may therefore be measured by the success and failure, the smoothness and roughness of … *the two-way translation between the language of individual/familial interests and the language of public interests* … the reforging of private concerns and desires into public issues; and, conversely, the reforging of issues of public concern into individual rights and duties."[29]

The current assault threatening higher education, and the humanities in particular, cannot be understood outside of the crisis of public values, ethics, youth, and democracy itself. This state of emergency must take "the social question" as its starting point, with its emphasis on addressing acute social problems, providing social protections for the disadvantaged, developing public spheres aimed at promoting the collective good, and protecting educational spheres that enable and deepen the knowledge, skills, and modes of agency necessary for a substantive democracy to flourish.[30] Putting the social question on the agenda for reclaiming higher education as a public good is an important challenge for the twenty-first century. In part, this means encouraging progressives, students, artists, academics, and others to examine those larger political, economic, and cultural forces that undermine all vestiges of solidarity, disdain any viable notion of the social state, and relegate all social protections to a form of pathology. There is also a need to develop those public spheres that provide the formative culture necessary for the production of critical agents, civic courage, and collective struggles against the myriad antidemocratic forces now threatening U.S. society.

What is especially urgent about the current threat to higher education is the increasing pace of the corporatization and militarization of the university, the squelching of academic freedom, the rise of an ever-increasing contingent of part-time faculty, and the view that students are basically consumers and faculty are providers of a saleable commodity such as a credential or a set of workplace skills. Not only has there been a massive increase in military funding within the university since 9/11 and a growing and chilling collaboration between higher education and the sixteen national intelligence agencies that make up the national security state, but also the breathtaking spread of corporate policies, values, and modes of governance throughout the realm of higher education.[31]

This is evident in a number of changes that are taking place throughout higher education. These changes include: a growing shift in governance away from faculty to administrations that largely define themselves in corporate terms; a growing restriction on academic freedom; a diminution of faculty rights; a growing army of part-time and nontenured faculty; the privileging of academic subjects and credentials tied to market-based principles; the rise of accountability measures that devalue critical thought and engaged scholarship; the blurring of lines between the university and the corporate world; the shaping of faculty research in the direction of corporate interests and priorities; and the appropriation of a corporate discourse in which students are viewed as customers, faculty as entrepreneurs, and university presidents as CEOs.[32] More striking still is the slow death of the university as a center of critique, vital source of civic education, and crucial public good. Or, to put it more specifically, the consequence of such dramatic transformations has resulted in the near-death of the university as a democratic public sphere. Many faculty are now demoralized as they increasingly lose their rights and power. Moreover, a weak faculty translates into one governed by fear rather than by shared responsibilities and one that is susceptible to labor-bashing tactics such as increased workloads, the casualization of labor, and the growing suppression of dissent.

A particularly distressing cause for alarm is the ongoing casualization of the academic labor force. As Ellen Schrecker puts it, this "is perhaps the most serious threat to American higher education today: the casualization of the academic labor force. More than 70 percent of all college-level instruction in the United States is now in the hands of contingent faculty members—part-time and full-time teachers with temporary contracts. The implications of that revolution (and it is a revolution) in the composition of the faculty—for the quality of its instruction, for the welfare of its students, and for the university's ability to carry out its traditional mission—can only be disastrous."[33] Unfortunately, demoralization in this period of job uncertainty, fear, and insecurity often translates less into moral outrage than into cynicism, accommodation, and a retreat into a sterile form of professionalism. What is also new is that faculty now find themselves staring into an abyss, either unwilling to address the current attacks on the university or befuddled over how the language of specialization and professionalization has cut them off from not only connecting their work to larger civic issues and social problems but also developing any meaningful relationships to a larger democratic polity.

As academics no longer feel compelled to address important political issues and social problems, they are less inclined to communicate with a larger public, uphold public values, or engage in a type of scholarship that is accessible to a broader audience.[34] Beholden to corporate interests, career building, and the insular discourses that accompany specialized scholarship, too many academics have become overly comfortable with the corporatization of the university and the new regimes of neoliberal governance. Chasing after grants, promotions, and conventional research outlets, many academics have retreated from larger public debates and refused to address urgent social problems. Assuming the role of the disinterested academic or the clever faculty star on the make, these so-called academic entrepreneurs simply reinforce the public's perception that they have become largely irrelevant. Incapable, if not unwilling, to defend the university as a democratic public sphere and a crucial site for learning how to think critically and act with civic courage, many academics have disappeared into a disciplinary apparatus that views the university not as a place to think but as a place to prepare students to be competitive in the global marketplace.

This is particularly disturbing, given the unapologetic turn that higher education has taken in its willingness to mimic corporate culture and ingratiate itself to the national security state.[35] Universities now face a growing set of challenges arising from budget cuts, diminishing quality, the downsizing of faculty, the militarization of research, and the revamping of the curriculum to fit the interests of the market. As I mentioned previously, many of the problems in higher education in the United States can be linked to low funding, the domination of universities by market mechanisms, the rise of for-profit colleges, the intrusion of the national security state, and the lack of faculty self-governance, all of which not only contradicts the culture and democratic value of higher education but also makes a mockery of the very meaning and mission of the university as a place both to think and to provide the formative culture and agents that make a democracy possible. Universities and colleges have been largely abandoned as democratic public spheres dedicated to providing a public service, expanding upon humankind's great intellectual and cultural achievements, and educating future generations to be able to confront the challenges of a global democracy. As the humanities and liberal arts are downsized, privatized, and commodified, higher education finds itself caught in the paradox of claiming to invest in the future of young people while offering them few intellectual, civic, and moral supports.

If the commercialization, commodification, and militarization of the university continues unabated, higher education will become yet another one of a number of institutions incapable of fostering critical inquiry, public debate, human acts of justice, and common deliberation. But the calculating logic of the corporate university does more than diminish the moral and political vision and practices necessary to sustain a vibrant democracy and an engaged notion of social agency. It also undermines the development of public spaces where matters of dissent, critical dialogue, social responsibility, and social justice are pedagogically valued and viewed as fundamental to providing students with the knowledge and skills necessary to address the problems facing the nation and the globe.[36] Such democratic public spheres are especially important to defend at a time when any space that produces "critical thinkers capable of putting existing institutions into question" is under siege by powerful economic and political interests.[37]

Higher education has a responsibility not only to search for the truth regardless of where it might lead, but also to educate students to make authority and power politically and morally accountable. Although questions regarding whether the university should serve *strictly* public rather than private interests no longer carry the weight of forceful criticism, as they did in the past, yet such questions are still crucial in addressing the purpose of higher education and what it might mean to imagine the university's full participation in public life as the protector and promoter of democratic values. What needs to be understood is that higher education might be one of the few public spheres left where knowledge, values, and learning offer a glimpse of the promise of education for nurturing public values, critical hope, and a substantive democracy. It might be the case that everyday life is increasingly organized around market principles; but confusing a market-determined society with democracy hollows out the legacy of higher education, whose deepest roots are moral, not commercial. This is a particularly important insight in a society where not only the free circulation of ideas is being replaced by ideas managed by the dominant media but critical ideas are increasingly viewed or dismissed as banal, if not reactionary.

As *New York Times* columnist Frank Rich has pointed out, the war against literacy and informed judgment is made abundantly clear in the populist rage sweeping across the country, a massive collective anger that "is aimed at the educated, not the wealthy."[38] Democracy places civic demands upon its citizens, and such demands point to the necessity of an education that is broad-based, critical, and supportive of meaningful civic values, participation in self-governance, and democratic leadership. Only through such a formative and critical educational culture can students learn how to become individual and social agents, rather than merely disengaged spectators, able both to think otherwise and to act upon civic commitments that demand a rethinking and reconstituting of basic power arrangements fundamental to promoting the common good and producing a meaningful democracy. It is important to insist that as educators we ask, again and again, how higher education can survive as a democratic public sphere in a society in which civic culture and modes of critical literacy collapse as it becomes more and more difficult to distinguish opinion and emotive outbursts from a sustained argument and logical reasoning.

Defending the humanities, as Terry Eagleton has recently argued, means more than offering an academic enclave for students to learn history, philosophy, art, and literature. It also means stressing how indispensable these fields of study are for all students if they are to be able to make any claim whatsoever on being critical and engaged individuals and social agents. But the humanities do far more. They also provide the knowledge, skills, social relations, and modes of pedagogy that constitute a formative culture in which the historical lessons of democratization can be learned, the demands of social responsibility can be thoughtfully engaged, the imagination can be expanded, and critical thought can be affirmed. As an adjunct of the academic-military-industrial complex, higher education has nothing to say about teaching students how to think for themselves in a democracy, how to think critically and engage with others, or how to address through the prism of democratic values the relationship between themselves and the larger world. We need a permanent and ongoing critical dialogue about the meaning and purpose of higher education, one in which academics are more than willing to move beyond the language of critique and a discourse of moral and political outrage, to a sustained individual and collective commitment to the ongoing re-creation of the university as a vital public sphere central to democracy itself.

Such a debate is important for defending higher education as a public good and funding it as a social right. Most importantly, such a debate represents a crucial political intervention regarding an entire generation's sense of the future and their role within it. Students are not consumers; they are first and foremost citizens of a potentially global democracy and as such should be provided with "the full range of human knowledge, understanding and creativity—and so ensure that [they] have the opportunity to develop their full intellectual and creative potential, regardless of family wealth."[39] As neoliberal ideology is enlisted to narrow the parameters and the purpose of higher education, it increasingly limits—through high tuition rates, technocratic modes of learning, the reduction of faculty to temporary workers, and authoritarian modes of governance—the ability of many young people to attend college while at the same time refusing to provide a critical education to those who do. It also reinforces modes of racial exclusion that fall primarily on those populations already marginalized through the blight of poverty, unemployment, and other massive inequalities. As the dynamics of austerity measures hollow out chances for young people to attend higher education, the burden of such measures falls largely upon poor students, but especially poor minorities of color, who increasingly are subjected to the disciplinary measures of the punishing state. Not enough faculty, students, parents, and others concerned about the fate of young people and democracy are mobilizing inside and outside of the university, willing and able to defend higher education as a public good and critical pedagogy as a moral and political practice that builds the capacity of young people to become engaged social agents.

Central to any viable, democratic view of higher education is the necessity to challenge the notion that the only value of education is to drive economic progress and acquisition in the interest of national prosperity. We must reject the idea that the university should be modeled after "a sterile Darwinian shark tank in which the only thing that matters is the bottom line."[40] We must also reconsider how the university in a post-9/11 era is being militarized and increasingly reduced to an adjunct of the growing national security state. The public has given up on the idea of either funding higher education or valuing it as a public good indispensable to the life of any viable democracy. This is all the more reason for academics to be at the forefront of a coalition of activists, public servants, and others by both rejecting the growing corporate management of higher education and developing a new discourse in which the university, and particularly the humanities, can be defended as a vital social and public institution in a democratic society. Once again, Ian Angus gets it right in arguing that:

> given the relatively recent transformation of the public university into a corporate environment, and given the still incomplete nature of this transformation, a memory of other practices and legitimations survives. In the era of the welfare state the publicly funded university was understood to play a public role in developing citizenship and social awareness— a role that shaped and overrode its economic function. This memory makes many people uncomfortable with the new corporate reality of the university. University culture is now torn between memories of better days that lead to a narrative of decline and despair and a new "realistic" resignation to the "fact" that the university is simply an economic institution no different from any other except insofar as making shoes is different from renting high rises.[41]

The university harbors memories of more democratic ideals, of possibilities in which its role as a democratic public sphere challenges rather than mirrors the reductionistic values and strategies of corporate power and neoliberal disciplinary practices. If academics cannot defend the university as a democratic public sphere, then who will? If we cannot or refuse to take the lead in joining with students, labor unions, public school teachers, artists, and other cultural workers in defending higher education as the most crucial institution in establishing the formative culture necessary for a thriving democracy, then we will turn the humanities, liberal arts, and the larger university over to a host of dangerously antidemocratic economic, political, cultural, and social forces. If liberal learning and the humanities collapse under the current assaults on higher education, we will witness the continued growth of a neoliberal state and the civic and democratic role of higher education, however tarnished, will disappear. Under such circumstances, higher education, and especially the humanities, will enter a death spiral unlike anything we have seen in the past. Not even a shadow of its former self, the university will become simply another institution, a set of vocational programs entirely at odds with imperatives of critical thought, dissent, social responsibility, and civic courage.

Defending the university means more than exhibiting a combination of critique and moral outrage. It means developing a critical and oppositional culture and collective movement within the university and joining with social movements outside of its now largely segregated walls. Reaching a broader public about the social and democratic character of higher education is crucial, especially because a large part of the public has given up on "the idea of educating people for democratic citizenship"[42] and viewing higher education as a public good. There is more at stake here than the deep responsibilities of academics to defend academic freedom, the tenure system, and faculty autonomy, however important they happen to be. The real issues are more expansive and speak to preserving the public character of higher education and recognizing that defending it as a public sphere is essential to the very existence of critical thinking, dissent, dialogue, engaged scholarship, and faculty autonomy. But it is also crucial to developing those formative cultures necessary to a vital democracy in which individual and social agents are needed to create social movements capable of large-scale economic restructuring. Amid the current structures of social and economic inequality, higher education can only become a remote outpost of resistance. To be a site of effective resistance and transformative possibility it has to link the crisis in higher education to the larger crisis in democracy. I think we can go further and suggest that we are at a turning point in U.S. history in which what is at stake is not limited to the possibility of higher education as a public good but extends to the very possibility of enlightened literacy, politics, and democracy itself. These may be dark times, as Hannah Arendt once warned, but they don't have to be, and that raises serious questions about what educators are going to do within the current historical climate to make sure that they do not succumb to the authoritarian forces circling the university, waiting for the resistance to stop and the lights to go out.

Notes

1. Toni Morrison, "How Can Values Be Taught in This University?" *Michigan Quarterly Review* (Spring 2001): 278.

2. Frank Rich, "Obama's Original Sin," *New York Magazine,* July 3, 2011, online at http://nymag.com/news/frank-rich/obama-economy/presidents-failure.

3. Matt Taibbi, "Why Isn't Wall Street in Jail?" *Rolling Stone,* February 16, 2011, online at http://www.rollingstone.com/politics/news/why-isnt-wall-street-in-jail-20110216.

4. Some useful sources on neoliberalism include: Lisa Duggan, *The Twilight of Equality* (Boston: Beacon Press, 2003); David Harvey, *A Brief History of Neoliberalism* (New York: Oxford University Press, 2005); Wendy Brown, *Edgework: Critical Essays on Knowledge and Politics* (Princeton, NJ: Princeton University Press, 2005); Alfredo Saad-Filho and Deborah Johnston, eds., *Neoliberalism: A Critical Reader* (London: Pluto Press, 2005); Neil Smith, *The Endgame of Globalization* (New York: Routledge, 2005); Aihwa Ong, *Neoliberalism as Exception: Mutations in Citizenship and Sovereignty* (Durham, NC: Duke University Press, 2006); Randy Martin, *An Empire of Indifference: American War and the Financial Logic of Risk Management* (Durham, NC: Duke University Press, 2007); Naomi Klein, *The Shock Doctrine: The Rise of Disaster Capitalism* (New York: Knopf, 2007); Henry A. Giroux, *Against the Terror of Neoliberalism* (Boulder, CO: Paradigm Publishers, 2008); David Harvey, *The Enigma of Capital and the Crisis of Capitalism* (New York: Oxford University Press, 2010); and Gerard Dumenil and Dominique Levy, *The Crisis of Neoliberalism* (Cambridge, MA: Harvard University Press, 2011).

5. Bauman, cited in Peter Beilharz, *Zygmunt Bauman: Dialectic of Modernity* (London: Sage, 2000), 158.

6. See, for example, Stanley Aronowitz, *Against Schooling: For an Education That Matters* (Boulder, CO: Paradigm Publishers, 2008); Christopher Newfield, *Unmaking the Public University* (Cambridge, MA: Harvard University Press, 2008); and Ellen Schrecker, *The Lost Soul of Higher Education* (New York: New Press, 2010). One of the most extensive compilations analyzing this assault can be found in Edward J. Carvalho and David B. Downing, eds., *Academic Freedom in the Post–9-11 Era* (New York: Palgrave, 2010); and Henry A. Giroux, *Education and the Crisis of Public Values* (New York: Peter Lang Publishing, 2011).

7. I take this issue up in great detail in Henry A. Giroux, *The University in Chains: Confronting the Military-Industrial-Academic Complex* (Boulder, CO: Paradigm Publishers, 2008). See also, Ellen Schrecker, *The Lost Soul of Higher Education* (New York: The New Press, 2010).

8. See, for example, Ellen Schrecker, *No Ivory Tower: McCarthyism and the Universities* (New York: Oxford University Press, 1986).

9. Classic examples would include: Alan Bloom, *The Closing of the American Mind* (New York: Simon and Schuster, 1988); Charles Sykes, *Profscam: Professors and the Demise of Higher Education* (Washington, DC: Regnery Press, 1988); Thomas Sowell, *Inside American Education: The Decline, The Deception, The Dogmas* (New York: The Free Press, 1993); and Martin Anderson, *Imposters in the Temple* (New York: Simon and Schuster, 1992).

10. For a history of student resistance both within and outside of the university, see Mark Edelman Boren, *Student Resistance: A History of the Unruly Subject* (New York: Routledge, 2001).

11. Ian Angus, *Love the Questions: University Education and Enlightenment* (Winnipeg: Arbeiter Ring Publishing, 2009).

12. This issue is taken up in great detail in Henry A. Giroux and Susan Searls Giroux, *Take Back Higher Education* (New York: Palgrave, 2004); and Susan Searls Giroux, *Between Race and Reason: Violence, Intellectual Responsibility, and the University to Come* (Stanford, CA: Stanford University Press, 2010).

13. See Jacques Derrida, "The Future of the Profession or the University without Condition (Thanks to the 'Humanities,' What *Could Take Place* Tomorrow)," in Tom Cohen, ed., *Jacques Derrida and the Humanities: A Critical Reader* (Cambridge: Cambridge University Press, 2001), 24–57.

14. Ellen Schrecker, *The Lost Soul of Higher Education* (New York: The New Press, 2010), 3.

15. Daniel Denvir, "Ayn Rand Indoctrination at American Universities, Sponsored by the Right Wing," *AlterNet,* May 24, 2011, online at http://www.alternet.org/teaparty/151066/ayn_rand_indoctrination_at_american_universities,_sponsored_by_the_right_wing/.

16. Vimal Patel, "A&M System Grades Faculty—By Bottom Line,"

TheEagle.com, September 1, 2010, online at http://www.theeagle .com/am/A-amp-amp-M-grades-faculty.

17. Ibid.

18. Ibid.

19. Scott Jaschik, "Faculty Pay 'by Applause Meter,'" *Inside Higher Ed,* January 13, 2009, online at http://www.insidehighered .com/news/2009/01/13/bonuspay.

20. Ibid.

21. See Isabelle Bruno and Christopher Newfield, "Can the Cognitariat Speak?" *E-Flux* no. 14, March 2010, online at http:// www.e-flux.com/journal/view/118/. See also Christopher Newfield, *Unmaking the Public University* (Cambridge, MA: Harvard University Press, 2008).

22. Graham Bowley, "The Academic-Industrial Complex," *New York Times,* July 31, 2010, online at http://query.nytimes .com/gst/fullpage.html?res=9E01EFDA143DF932A3575BC0A 9669D8B63&ref=graham_bowley&pagewanted=4.

23. Cited in ibid.

24. For an interesting critique of this subject, see the special issue of *The Nation* called "Out of Reach: Is College Only for the Rich?" (June 29, 2009).

25. Zygmunt Bauman, *Liquid Fear* (London: Polity Press, 2006).

26. For an interesting discussion of this issue, see Gayatri Chakravorty Spivak, "Changing Reflexes: Interview with Gayatri Chakravorty Spivak," *Works and Days* 55/56 (2010): 1–21. I have also taken up this issue in a number of books. See most recently Henry A. Giroux, *Youth in a Suspect Society* (New York: Palgrave, 2009); and Henry A. Giroux, *On Critical Pedagogy* (New York: Continuum Press, 2011).

27. Sheldon Wolin, "Political Theory: From Vocation to Invocation," in Jason Frank and John Tambornino, eds., *Vocations of Political Theory* (Minneapolis: University of Minnesota Press, 2000), 4.

28. C. Wright Mills, *The Sociological Imagination* (Oxford: Oxford University Press, 2000).

29. Zygmunt Bauman, *Collateral Damage: Social Inequalities in a Global Age* (London: Polity Press, 2011), 11.

30. Tony Judt, *Ill Fares the Land* (New York: Penguin, 2010).

31. I take this issue up in great detail in Henry A. Giroux, *The University in Chains: Confronting the Military-Industrial-Academic Complex* (Boulder, CO: Paradigm Publishers, 2007).

32. See Peter Seybold's excellent analysis of the corporate university in Peter Seybold, "The Struggle Against the Corporate Takeover of the University," *Socialism and Democracy* 22:1 (March 2008): 1–11.

33. Ellen Schrecker, *The Lost Soul of Higher Education* (New York: The New Press, 2010), 3.

34. This argument has been made against academics for quite some time, though it has been either forgotten or conveniently ignored by many faculty. See, for example, various essays in C. Wright Mills, "The Powerless People: The Role of the Intellectual in Society," in C. Wright Mills, *The Politics of Truth: Selected Writings of C. Wright Mills* (Oxford: Oxford University Press, 2008), 13–24; Edward Said, *Humanism and Democratic Criticism* (New York: Columbia University Press, 2004); and Henry A. Giroux and Susan Searls Giroux, *Take Back Higher Education* (New York: Palgrave, 2004).

35. On the university's relationship with the national security state, see David Price, "How the CIA Is Welcoming Itself Back onto American University Campuses: Silent Coup," *CounterPunch*, April 9–11, 2010, online at http://www.counterpunch.org/price04092010.html. See also Nick Turse, *How the Military Invades Our Everyday Lives* (New York: Metropolitan Books, 2008); and Henry A. Giroux, *The University in Chains: Confronting the Military-Industrial-Academic Complex* (Boulder, CO: Paradigm Publishers, 2007).

36. For an excellent study on the metamorphosis of the corporate university and its stultifying managerialism, see Gaye Tuchman, *Wannabe U: Inside the Corporate University* (Chicago: University of Chicago Press, 2009).

37. Cornelius Castoriadis, "Democracy as Procedure and Democracy as Regime," *Constellations* 4:1 (1997): 5.

38. Frank Rich, "Could She Reach the Top in 2012? You Betcha," *New York Times*, November 20, 2010, WK8.

39. Stefan Collini, "Browne's Gamble," *London Review of Books*, vol. 32, no. 21, November 4, 2010, online at http://www.lrb.co.uk/v32/n21/stefan-collini/brownes-gamble.

40. Stephen Holden, "Perils of the Corporate Ladder: It Hurts When You Fall," *New York Times*, December 10, 2010, C9.

41. Ian Angus, "Academic Freedom in the Corporate University," in Mark Cote, Richard J. F. Day, and Greig de Peuter, eds., *Utopian Pedagogy: Radical Experiments against Neoliberal Globalization* (Toronto: University of Toronto Press, 2007), 65.

42. David Glenn, "Public Higher Education Is 'Eroding from All Sides,' Warn Political Scientists," *Chronicle of Higher Education*, September 2, 2010, online at http://chronicle.com/article/Public-Higher-Education-Is/124292/.

◇

Index

Judt, Tony, 34, 40, 51, 57, 73

Kane, Mike, 8
Kingston, Jack, 92–93
Klee, Paul, 34–35
Koch brothers, 124
Kohn, Sally, 82
Krauthammer, Charles, 91

Lacey, Marc, 44
language: of democracy, 127–28; on social state, 50–52
Leadership Institute, 13
Lerner, Michael, 118
Libya, 2
Limbaugh, Rush, 92
Lowenthal, Leo, 19
Lynch, Peter L., 97

Maher, Bill, 92
Mahir, Ahmed, 1
market fundamentalism: versus social state, 39. *See also* economic Darwinism
Martin, Courtney, 11, 30n28
Marx, Karl, 5
Mbembe, Achille, 39
McKinney, Michael D., 125
McMahon, Linda, 93
media: conservative, 61; and democracy, 63–64; and inequality, 49; intellectuals and, 118. *See also* new media
Michigan, 15
militarization. *See* war
Mills, C. Wright, 68–70, 99; on organized irresponsibility, 51–52; on public intellectuals, 104–5; on sociological imagination, 65–66, 127
morality: Bauman on, 46; forgetting and, 44, 66; neoliberalism and, 121–22

Morocco, 6
Morrison, Toni, 120
Moyers, Bill, 118

Nelson, Cary, 125
neoliberalism: and culture, 57; effects of, 121; Fukuyama and, 87n35; and higher education, 17, 100; ideology of, 36, 41–42; and morality, 121–22; and new media, 79–80; and politics, 5; public pedagogy and, 72; resistance to, 106; and social, 6, 63–65; sources on, 84n4, 136n4; youth movements and, 3–4, 6–7, 11, 19–20. *See also under* economic
new media: and neoliberalism, 41–42; possibilities of, 76, 78, 83; and public values, 74–84; and resistance, 26; and youth movements, 10. *See also* media

Obama administration, 43, 96, 120
one percent. *See* financial elite
O'Reilly, Bill, 92

Parker, Mark G., 97
pedagogy: and formative cultures, 68–72. *See also* education; public pedagogy
Pell Grants, 15, 17
People for the American Way, 12
permanent education, term, 69
Pilger, John, 4
politics: and austerity, 7–8; of economic Darwinism, 95; and higher education, 104; Mbembe on, 39; neoliberalism and, 5;

◇

About the Author

A prominent American social critic, Henry A. Giroux holds the Global TV Network Chair at McMaster University in Canada. He is the author most recently of *Politics After Hope: Obama and the Crisis of Youth, Race, and Democracy* and *Hearts of Darkness: Torturing Children in the War on Terror.*